HANDY PROJECTS
FOR BOYS

HANDY PROJECTS FOR BOYS

More Than 200 Projects Including Skis,
Hammocks, Paper Balloons, Wrestling
Mats, and Microscopes

Editors of *Popular Mechanics Press*

SKYHORSE PUBLISHING

Skyhorse Publishing books may be purchased in bulk at special discounts for sales promotion, corporate gifts, fund-raising, or educational purposes. Special editions can also be created to specifications. For details, contact the Special Sales Department, Skyhorse Publishing, 307 West 36th Street, 11th Floor, New York, NY 10018 or info@skyhorsepublishing.com.

Skyhorse® and Skyhorse Publishing® are registered trademarks of Skyhorse Publishing, Inc.®, a Delaware corporation.

www.skyhorsepublishing.com

10 9 8 7 6 5 4 3 2 1
Library of Congress Cataloging-in-Publication Data is available on file.

ISBN: 978-1-62873-774-5

Printed in the United States of America

HANDY PROJECTS
FOR BOYS

TABLE OF CONTENTS

TABLE OF CONTENTS

CAMP ACTIVITIES FOR THE GREAT OUTDOORS

A Guitar That is Easy to Make

A guitar having straight lines, giving it an old-fashioned appearance, can be made by the home mechanic, and if care is taken in selecting the material, and having it thoroughly seasoned, the finished instrument will have a fine tone. The sides, ends and bottom are made of hard wood, preferably hard maple, and the top should be made of a thoroughly seasoned piece of soft pine. The dimensioned pieces required are as follows:

1 Top, ³⁄₁₆ by 14 by 17 in.
1 Bottom, ³⁄₁₆ bys 14 by 17 in.
2 Sides, ³⁄₁₆ by 3 ⅝ by 16¾ in.
1 End, ³⁄₁₆ by 3 ⅝ by 13 ¹⁄₈₆ in.
1 End, ³⁄₁₆ by 3 ⅝ by 9 ⅝ in.
1 Neck, 1 by 2 ⁵⁄₁₆ by 18½ in.
1 Fingerboard, ³⁄₁₆ by 2 ⅝ by 16 in.

Cut the fingerboard tapering and fasten pieces cut from hatpins with small wire staples for frets. All dimensions for cutting and setting are shown in the sketch. The neck is cut tapering from G to F and from J to F, with the back side rounding. A draw-knife is the proper tool for shaping the neck. Cut a piece of hard wood, ¼ in. square and 1⅞ in. long, and glue

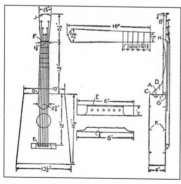

Details of Guitar

it to the neck at F. Glue the fingerboard to the neck and hold it secure with clamps while the glue sets.

The brace at D is 1 in. thick, cut to any shape desired. The sides are glued together and then the front is glued on them. Place some heavy weights on top and give the glue time to dry. Fasten pieces of soft wood in the corners for braces. Glue the neck to the box, making it secure by the addition of a carriage bolt at A. A small block C is glued to the end to reinforce it for the bolt. Glue strips of soft wood, as shown by K, across the front and back to strengthen them. The back is then glued on and the outside smoothed with sandpaper.

Make the bottom bridge by using an old hatpin or wire of the same size for E secured with pin staples. Glue the bridge on the top at a place that will make the distance from the bridge F to the bottom bridge E just 24 in. This dimension and those for the frets should be made accurately. Six holes, $\frac{3}{16}$ in. in diameter, are drilled in the bottom bridge for pins. The turning plugs B and strings can be purchased at any music store.— Contributed by J. H. Stoddard, Carbondale, Pa.

A MONOPLANE WEATHER VANE

The toy windmill or weather vane shown in the sketch is made to represent a Blériot monoplane. The propeller is turned by the wind. The frame is made of heavy wire and connected with straps of tin. The construction is plainly shown in the illustration. The windmill vane can be made in any size to suit the builder.— Contributed by W. C. Bliss, St. Louis, Missouri.

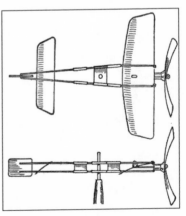

Wire and Sheet-Metal Vane

GREASING THE FRONT WHEELS OF AN AUTOMOBILE

The front wheel bearings of an automobile can be greased without removing the wheels in the following manner: Remove the hub caps and fill them with heavy grease and then screw them in place. Continue this operation until the grease is forced between all the bearings and out through the small clearance on the opposite side of the wheels. This should be done at least once every month to keep bearings well lubricated and free from grit. Dirt cannot enter a well filled bearing as easily as muddy water can enter a dry bearing.—Contributed by Chas. E. Frary, Norwalk, O.

Mold on wallpaper can be removed at once by applying a solution of 1 part salicylic acid in 4 parts of 95-percent alcohol.

HOW TO CROSS A STREAM ON A LOG

When crossing a water course on a fence rail or small log, do not face up or down the stream and walk sideways, for a wetting is the inevitable result. Instead, fix the eye on the opposite shore and walk steadily forward. Then if a mishap comes, you will fall with one leg and arm encircling the bridge.—C. C. S.

HOW TO MAKE A FLINT ARROWHEAD

If you live where flints abound, possess the requisite patience and the knack of making things, you can, with the crudest of tools and a little practice, chip out as good arrowheads as any painted savage that ever drew a bow.

Select a piece of straight-grained flint as near the desired shape as possible. It may be both longer and wider than the finished arrow but it should not be any thicker. The side, edge and end views of a suitable fragment are shown in Fig. 1. Hold the piece with one edge

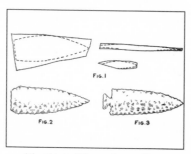

The Stone Chipped into Shape

or end resting on a block of wood and strike the upper edge lightly with a hammer, a small boulder or anything that comes handy until the piece assumes the shape shown in Fig. 2.

The characteristic notches shown in the completed arrow, Fig. 3, are chipped out by striking the piece lightly at the edge of an old hatchet or a heavy flint held at right angles to the edge of the arrow. These heads can be made so that they cannot be arrowheads.—Contributed by B. Orlando Taylor, Cross Timbers, Mo.

Fig. 1

Paper Balloon

How to Make Paper Balloons

Balloons made spherical, or designed after the regular aeronaut's hot-air balloon, are the best kind to make. Those having an odd or unusual shape will not make good ascensions, and in most cases the paper will catch fire from the torch and burn before they have flown very far. The following description is for making a tissue-paper balloon about 6 ft. high.

The paper may be selected in several colors, and the gores cut from these, pasted in alternately, will produce a pretty array of colors when the balloon is in flight. The shape of a good balloon is shown in Fig. 1. The gores for a 6-ft. balloon should be about 8 ft. long or about one-third longer than the height of the balloon. The widest part of each gore is 16 in. The widest place should be 53½ in. from the bottom end, or a little over half way from the bottom to the top. The bottom of the gore is one-third the width of the widest point. The dimensions and shape of each gore are shown in Fig. 2.

The balloon is made up of 13 gores pasted together, using about ½-in. lap on the edges. Any good paste will do—one that is made up of flour and water well cooked will serve the purpose. If the gores have been put together right, the pointed ends will close up the top entirely and the wider bottom ends will leave an opening about 20 in. in diameter. A light wood hoop having the same diameter as the opening is pasted to the bottom end of the gores. Two cross wires are fastened to the hoop, as shown in Fig. 3. These are to hold the wick ball, Fig. 4, so it will hang as shown in Fig. 5. The wick ball is made by winding wicking around a wire, having the ends bent into hooks as shown.

The balloon is filled with hot air in a manner similar to that used with the ordinary cloth balloon. A small trench or fireplace is made of brick having a chimney over which the mouth of the paper balloon is placed. Use fuel that will make heat with very little smoke. Hold the balloon so it will not catch fire from the flames coming out of the chimney. Have some alcohol ready to pour on the wick ball, saturating it thoroughly. When the balloon is well filled carry it away from the fireplace, attach the wick ball to the cross wire and light it

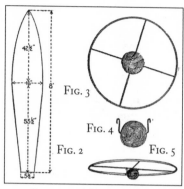

Pattern and Parts to Make Balloon

In starting the balloon on its flight, take care that it leaves the ground as nearly upright as possible.—Contributed by R. E. Staunton.

KEEPING FOOD COOL IN CAMPS

Camps and suburban homes located where ice is hard to get can be provided with a cooling arrangement herein described that will make a good substitute for the icebox. A barrel is sunk in the ground in a shady place, allowing plenty of space about the outside to fill in with gravel. A quantity of small stones and sand is first put in wet. A box is placed in the hole over the top of the barrel and filled in with clay or earth well tamped. The porous condition of the gravel drains the surplus water after a rain.

The end of the barrel is fitted with a light cover and a heavy door hinged to the box. A small portion of damp sand is sprinkled on the bottom of the barrel. The covers should be left open occasionally to prevent mold and to remove any bad air that may have collected from the contents.—Contributed by F. Smith, La Salle, Ill.

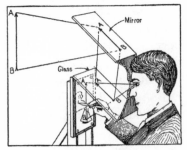

Drawing with the Aid of
Reflecting Glasses

LANDSCAPE DRAWING MADE EASY

With this device anyone, no matter how little his artistic ability may be, can draw accurately and quickly any little bit of scenery or other subject and get everything in the true perspective and in the correct proportion.

No lens is required for making this camera—just a plain mirror set at an angle of 45 deg., with a piece of ordinary glass underneath, a screen with a peek hole and a board for holding the drawing paper. The different parts may be fastened together by means of a box frame, or may be hinged together to allow folding up when carrying and a good tripod of heavy design should be used for supporting it. In order to get the best results the screen should be blackened on the inside and the eyepiece should be blackened on the side next to the eye. A piece of black cardboard placed over the end of the eyepiece and perforated with a pin makes an excellent peek hole.

In operation the rays of light coming from any given object, such as the arrow AB, strike the inclined mirror and are reflected downward. On striking the inclined glass a portion of the light is again reflected and the rays entering the eye of the operator produce the virtual image on the paper as shown. The general outlines may be sketched in quickly, leaving the details to be worked up later. This arrangement may be used for interior work when the illumination is good.

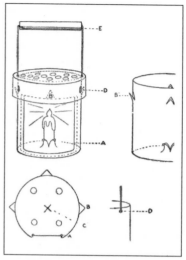

Lantern Made of Old Cans

MAKESHIFT CAMPER'S LANTERN

While out camping, our only lantern was accidentally smashed beyond repair and it was necessary for us to devise something that would take its place. We took an empty tomato can and cut out the tin 3 in. wide for a length extending from a point 2 in. below the top and to within ¼ in. of the bottom. Each side of the cut-out A was bent inward in the shape of a letter S, in which was placed a piece of glass. Four V-shaped notches were cut as shown at B near the top of the can and their points turned outward. A slit was cut in the bottom, shaped as shown at C, and the pointed ends thus formed were turned up to make a place for holding the base of a candle. A larger can was secured and the bottom perforated. This was turned over the top of the other can. A heavy wire was run through the perforations and a short piece of broom handle used to make a bail.—Contributed by Maurice Baudier, New Orleans, La.

MEASURING THE HEIGHT OF A TREE

"Near the end of the season our boy announced the height of our tall maple tree to be 33 ft.

"'Why, how do you know?' was the general question.

"'Measured it.'

"'How?'

"'Foot rule and yardstick.'

"'You didn't climb that tall tree?' his mother asked anxiously.

"'No'm; I found the length of the shadow and measured that.'

"'But the length of the shadow changes.'

"'Yes'm; but twice a day the shadows are just as long as the things themselves. I've been trying it all summer. I drove a stick into the ground, and when its shadow was just as long as the stick I knew that the shadow of the tree would

Method of Applying the Triangle Measure

be just as long as the tree, and that's 33 ft.'"

The above paragraphs appeared in one of the daily papers which come to our office. The item was headed, "A clever Boy." Now we do not know who this advertised boy was, but we knew quite as clever a boy, one who could have got the approximate height of the tree without waiting for the sun to shine at a particular angle or to shine at all for that matter. The way boy No. 2 went about the same problem was this: He got a stick and planted it in the ground and then cut it off just at the level of his eyes. Then he went out and took a look at the tree and made a rough estimate of the tree's height in his mind, and judging the same distance along the ground from the tree trunk, he planted his stick in the ground. Then he lay down on his back with his feet against the standing stick and looked at the top of the tree over the stick.

If he found the top of stick and tree did not agree he tried a new position and kept at it until he could just see the tree top over the end of the upright stick. Then all he had to do was to measure along the ground to where his eye had been when lying down and that gave him the height of the tree.

The point about this method is that the boy and stick made a right-angled triangle with boy for base, stick for perpendicular, both of the same length, and the "line of sight" the hypotenuse or long line of the triangle. When he got into the position which enabled him to just see the tree top over the top of the stick he again had a right-angled triangle with tree as perpendicular, his eye's distance away from the trunk, the base, and the line of sight the hypotenuse. He could measure the base line along the ground and knew it must equal the vertical height, and he could do this without reference to the sun. It was an ingenious application of the well known properties of a right-angled triangle.—Railway and Locomotive Engineer.

SPRINGBOARD FOR SWIMMERS

A good springboard adds much to the fun of swimming. The boards are generally made

so that the plank will bend, being dressed down thin at one end and fastened. The thinness of the plank, or an insecure fastening, causes many a plank to snap in two or come loose from its fastenings in a short time.

The accompanying sketch shows the method of constructing a springboard that does not depend upon the bending of the wood for its spring. It is made of a plank, 2 in. thick and from 14 to 16 ft. long, one end of which is secured with a hinge arrangement having a U-shaped rod whose ends are held with nuts. On each edge of the board, at the lower end, are fastened two pieces of strap iron, each about 1ft. long and with the lower

Buggy Springs Used beneath
the Board

ends drilled to fit the horizontal of the U-shaped rod.

Secure a pair of light buggy springs from a discarded rig and attach them to the ends of a square bar of iron having a length equal to the width of the plank. Fasten this to the plank with bolts, as shown in the sketch. Should the springs be too high they can be moved forward.—Contributed by John Blake, Franklin, Mass.

Pressure Experiments

THE DIVING BOTTLE

This is a very interesting and easily performed experiment illustrating the transmission of pressure by liquids. Take a wide-mouthed bottle and fill almost full of water; then into this bottle place, mouth downward, a small vial or bottle having just enough air in the bottle to keep it barely afloat. Put a sheet of rubber over the mouth of the large bottle, draw the edge down over the neck and wrap securely with a piece of string thus forming a tightly stretched diaphragm over the top. When a finger is pressed on the rubber the small bottle will slowly descend until the pressure is released when the small bottle will ascend. The moving of the small bottle is caused by the pressure transmitted through the water, thus causing the volume of air in the small tube to decrease and the bottle to descend and ascend when released as the air increases to the original volume.

This experiment can be performed with a narrow-necked bottle, provided the bottle is wide, but not very thick. Place the small bottle in as before, taking care not to have too much air in the bottom. If the cork is adjusted properly, the bottle may be held in the hand and the sides pressed with the fingers, thus causing the small bottle to descend and ascend at will. If the small bottle used is opaque, or an opaque tube such as the cap of a fountain pen, many puzzling effects may be obtained.—Contributed by John Shahan, Auburn, Ala.

BOYS REPRESENTING THE CENTAUR

This is a diversion in which two boys personate a Centaur, a creature of Greek mythology, half man and half horse. One of the players stands erect and the other behind him in a stooping position with his hands upon the first player's hips, as shown in Fig. 1. The second player is covered over with a shawl or table cover which is pinned around the waist of the first player. A tail made of strips of cloth or paper is pinned to the rear end of the cover. The first player should hold a bow and arrow and have a cloak thrown loosely over his shoulder as shown in Fig. 2. Imitation hoofs of pasteboard may be made and fastened over the shoes.

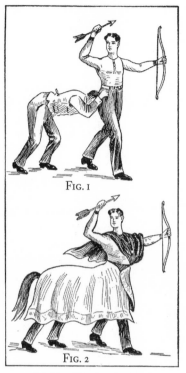

FIG. 1

FIG. 2

Making Up the Centaur

BUILDING A HOUSE IN A TREE TOP

The accompanying photograph shows a small house built in a tree top 20 ft. from the ground. The house is 5 ft. wide, 5 ft. 1 in. long, and 6ft. 6 in. high. A small platform, 2 ft. wide, is built on the front. Three windows are provided,

Lofty Sentry Box for Guarding Watermelon Patch

one for each side, and a door in front. The entrance is made through a trap door in the floor of the house. This house was constructed by a boy 14 years old and made for the purpose of watching over a melon patch.—Contributed by Mack Wilson, Columbus, O.

CARDBOARD SPIRAL TURNED BY HEAT

A novel attraction for a window display can be made from a piece of stiff cardboard cut in a spiral as shown in Fig. 1. The cardboard should be about 7 or 8 in. in diameter. Tie a piece of string to the center point of the spiral and fasten it so as to hang over a gas jet, Fig. 2. A small swivel must be put in the string at the top or near the cardboard,

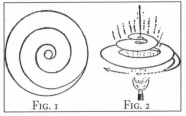

Spiral Cut from Cardboard

if it is desired to have the spiral run for any length of time. The cardboard will spin around rapidly and present quite an attraction.—Contributed by Harry Szerlip, Brooklyn, N. Y.

CENTER OF GRAVITY EXPERIMENT

This experiment consists of suspending a pail of water from a stick placed upon a table as shown in the accompanying sketch. In order to accomplish

this experiment, which seems impossible, it is necessary to place a stick, A, of sufficient length, between the end of the stick on the table and the bottom of the pail. This makes the center of gravity somewhere near the middle of the stick on the table thus holding the pail as shown.

COIN AND CARD ON THE FIRST FINGER

This is a simple trick that many can do at the first attempt, while others will fail time after time. It is a good trick to spring upon a company casually if you have practiced it beforehand. A playing card is balanced on the tip of the forefinger and a penny placed on top immediately over the finger end, as shown in the sketch. With the right-hand forefinger and thumb strike the edge of the card sharply. If done properly the card will fly away, leaving the penny poised on the finger end.

CONNECTING UP BATTERIES TO GIVE ANY VOLTAGE

Referring to the illustration: A is a five-point switch (may be home-made); B is a one-point switch, and C and C^1 are binding posts. When switch B is closed and A is on No. 1, you have the current of one battery; when A is on No. 2 you receive the current from two batteries; when on No. 3, from there batteries; when on No.4, from four batteries, and when on No. 5, from five batteries. More batteries may be connected to each point of switch B.

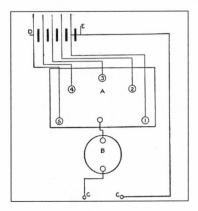

I have been using the same method for my water rheostat (homemade). I have the jars of water where the batteries are and the current coming in at a and b.—Contributed by Eugene F. Tuttle, Jr., Newark, Ohio.

EXPERIMENTS

A Microscope Without a Lens

BY E. W. DAVIS

Nearly everyone has heard of the pin-hole camera, but the fact that the same principle can be used to make a microscope, having a magnifying power of 8 diameters (64 times) will perhaps be new to some readers.

To make this lensless microscope, procure a wooden spool,

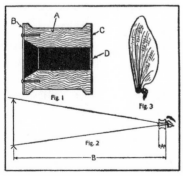

Detail of Lensless Microscope

A (a short spool, say ½ or ¾ in. long, produces a higher magnifying power), and enlarge the bore a little at one end. Then blacken the inside with india ink and allow it to dry. From a piece of thin transparent celluloid or mica, cut out a small disk, B, and fasten to the end having the enlarged bore, by means of brads. On the other end glue a piece of thin black cardboard, C, and at the center, D, make a small hole with the point of a fine needle. It is very important that the hole D should be very small, otherwise the image will be blurred.

To use this microscope, place a small object on the transparent disk, which may be moistened to make the object adhere, and look through the hole D. It is necessary to have a strong light to get good results, and, as

15

in all microscopes of any power, the object should be of a transparent nature.

The principle on which this instrument works is illustrated in Fig. 2. The apparent diameter of an object is inversely proportional to its distance from the eye, i. e., if the distance is reduced to one-half, the diameter will appear twice as large; if the distance is reduced to one-third, the diameter will appear three times as large, and so on. As the nearest distance at which the average person can see an object clearly is about 6 in., it follows that the diameter of an object ¾ in. from the eye would appear 8 times the normal size. The object would then be magnified 8 diameters, or 64 times. (The area would appear 64 times as large.) But an object ¾ in. from the eye appears so blurred that none of the details are discernible, and it is for this reason that the pin-hole is employed.

Viewed through this microscope, a fly's wing appears as large as a person's hand, held at arm's length, and has the general appearance shown in Fig. 3. The mother of vinegar examined in the same way is seen to be swarming with a mass of wriggling little worms, and may possibly cause the observer to abstain from all salads forever after. An innocent-looking drop of water, in which hay has been soaking for several days, reveals hundreds of little infusoria, darting across the field in every direction. These and hundreds of other interesting objects may be observed in this little instrument, which costs little or nothing to make.

EQUILIBRATOR FOR MODEL AEROPLANES

On one of my model aeroplanes, I placed an equilibrator to keep it balanced. The device was attached to a crosspiece fastened just below the propeller between the main frame uprights. A stick was made to swing on a bolt in the center of the crosspiece to which was attached a weight at the lower end and two lines connecting the ends of the planes at the upper end. These are shown in Fig. 1. When the aeroplane tips, as shown in Fig. 2, the

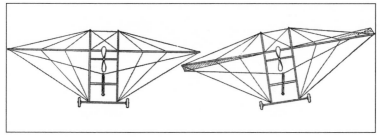

Wraping the Aeroplane Wings

weight draws the lines to warp the plane so it will right itself automatically.—Contributed by Louis J. Day, Floral Park, N. Y.

FOURTH-OF-JULY CATAPULT

Among the numerous exciting amusements in which boys may participate during the Fourth-of-July celebration is to make a cannon that will shoot life-sized dummies dressed in old clothes. Building the cannon, as described in the following, makes it safe to fire and not dangerous to others, provided care is taken to place it at an angle of 45 deg. and not to fire when anyone is within its range. The powder charge is in the safest form possible, as it is fired with a blow from a hammer instead of lighting a fuse. If the cannon is made according to directions, there cannot possibly be any explosion.

The materials used in the construction of the catapult may be found in almost any junk pile, and the only work required, outside of what can be done at home, is to have a few threads cut on the pieces of pipe. The fittings can be procured ready to attach, except for drilling a hole for the firing pin.

Secure a piece of common gas pipe, 4 to 6 in. in diameter, the length being from 18 to 24 in. Old pipe may be used if it is straight. Have a machinist cut threads on the outside of one end, as shown in Fig. 1, and fit an iron cap, Fig. 2, tightly on the threaded end of the pipe. The cap is drilled and tapped in the center for a 1-in. pipe.

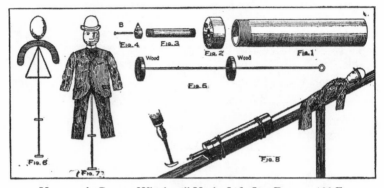

Homemade Cannon Which will Hurl a Life-Size Dummy 100 Ft. through the Air

Thread both ends of a 1-in. pipe that is 4 in. long, Fig. 3, and turn one end securely into the threaded hole of the cap. This pipe should project ¼ in. inside of the cap. Fit a cap, Fig. 4, loosely on the other end of the 1-in. pipe. A hole is drilled into the center of this small cap just large enough to receive a 6-penny wire nail, B, Fig. 4.

This completes the making of the cannon and the next step is to construct a dummy which can be dressed in old clothes. Cut out two round blocks of wood from hard pine or oak that is about 3 in. thick, as shown in Fig. 5. The diameter of these blocks should be about ⅛ in. less than the hole in the cannon, so they will slide easily.

In the center of each block bore a ¼-in. hole. Secure an iron rod, about 4 ft. long, and make a ring at one end and thread 4 in. of the other. Slip one of the circular blocks on the rod and move it up toward the ring about 14 in. Turn a nut on the threads, stopping it about 3½ in. from the end of the rod. Slip the other circular piece of wood on the rod and up against the nut, and turn on another nut to hold the wooden block firmly in its place at the end of the rod. If the rod is flattened at the place where the upper block is located, it will hold tight. These are shown in Fig. 5. Take some iron wire about ⅛ in. in diameter and make a loop at the top of the rod for the head. Wire this loop to the ring made in the rod and make the head about this loop by using canvas or gunny cloth sewed up forming a bag into which stuffed either excelsior, paper or hay. The arms are made by lashing with fine wire or strong hemp, a piece of wood 1 in. square and 20 in. long, or one cut in the shape shown in Fig. 6, to the rod. Place the wood arms close to the bottom of the head. Make a triangle of wire and fasten it and the cross arm securely to the top of the rod to keep them from slipping down. A false face, or one painted on white cloth, can be sewed on the stuffed bag. An old coat and trousers are put on the frame to complete the dummy. If the clothing is not too heavy and of white material so much the better. To greatly increase the spectacular flight through the air, a number of different colored streamers, 6 or 8 in. wide and several feet in length made from bunting, can be attached about the waist of the dummy. The complete dummy should not weigh more than 6 lb.

The cannon is mounted on a board with the cap end resting against a cleat which is securely nailed to the board and then bound tightly with a rope as shown in Fig. 8. Lay one end of the board on the ground and place the other on boxes or supports sufficiently high to incline it at an angle of about 45 deg. Enough of the board should project beyond the end of the cannon on which to lay the dummy. When completed as described, it is then ready to load and fire. Clear away everyone in front and on each side of the cannon, as the dummy will fly from 50 to 100 ft. and no one must be in range of its flight. This is important, as the rod of the frame holding the clothes will penetrate a board at short range. An ordinary shot gun cartridge of the paper shell type is used for the charge and it must be loaded with powder only. Coarse black powder is the best, but any size will do. When loading the rod with the wooden blocks, on which the dummy is attached, do not place the end block against the breech end of the cannon, leave about 2 or 3 in. between the end of the cannon and the block. Insert the cartridge in the 1-in. pipe. The cartridge should fit the pipe snug, which it will do if the proper size is secured. Screw on the firing-cap, insert the wire nail firing-pin until it rests against the firing-cap of the cartridge. If the range is clear the firing may be done by giving the nail a sharp rap with a hammer. A loud report will follow with a cloud of smoke and the dummy will be seen flying through the air, the arms, legs and streamers fluttering, which presents a most realistic and life-like appearance. The firing may be repeated any number of times in the same manner.

Volcano in Action

How to Make a Miniature Volcano

A toy volcano that will send forth flames and ashes with lava streaming down its sides in real volcanic action can be made by any boy without any more danger than firing an ordinary fire-cracker. A mound of sand or earth is built up about 1 ft. high in the shape of a volcano. Roll up a piece of heavy paper,

making a tube 5 in. long and 1½ in. in diameter. This tube of paper as placed in the top of the mound by first setting it upon a flat sheet of paper and building up the sand or earth about the sides until it is all covered excepting the top opening. This is to keep all dampness away from the mixture to be placed within.

A fuse from a fire-cracker, or one made by winding some powder in tissue paper, is placed in the paper tube of the volcano with one end extending over the edge. Get some potash from a drug store and be sure to state the purpose for which it is wanted, as there are numerous kinds of potash that will not be suitable. An equal amount of sugar is mixed with the potash and placed in the paper tube. On top of this put a layer of pure potash and on this pour some gun powder. This completes the volcano and it only remains for the fuse to be lighted and action will begin with an explosion which sends fire, smoke and sparks upward. Flames will follow and the lava pours flown the sides of the mound.

How to Make a Telescope

With a telescope like the one here described, made with his own hands, a farmer boy not many years ago discovered a comet which had escaped the watchful eyes of any astronomers.

First, get two pieces of plate glass, 6 in. square and 1 in. thick, and break the corners off to make them round, grinding the rough edges on a grindstone. Use a barrel to work on, and fasten one glass on the top of it in the center by driving three small nails at the sides to hold it in place. Fasten, with pitch, a round 4-in. block of wood in the center on one side of the other glass to serve as a handle.

Use wet grain emery for coarse grinding. Take a pinch and spread it evenly on the glass which is on the barrel, then take the glass with the handle and move it back and forth across the lower glass, while walking around the barrel; also rotate the glass, which is necessary to make it grind evenly. The upper glass or speculum always becomes concave, and the under glass or tool convex.

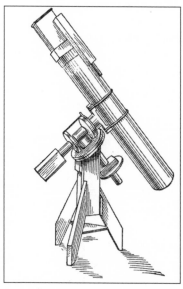

Homemade Telescope

Work with straight strokes 5 or 6 in. in length; after working 5 hours hold the speculum in the sunshine and throw the rays of the sun onto a paper; where the rays come to a point gives the focal length. If the glass is not ground enough to bring the rays to a point within 5 ft., the coarse grinding must be continued, unless a longer focal length is wanted.

Have ready six large dishes, then take 2 lb. flour emery and mix in 12 qt. of water; immediately turn the water into a clean dish and let settle 30 seconds; then turn it into another dish and let settle 2 minutes, then 8 minutes, 30 minutes and 90 minutes, being careful not to turn off the coarser emery which has settled. When dry, turn the emery from the 5 jars into 5 separate bottles, and label. Then take a little of the coarsest powder, wetting it to the consistency of cream, and spread on the glass, work as before (using short straight strokes 1½ or 2 in.) until the holes in the glass left by the grain emery are ground out; next use the finer grades until the pits left by each coarser grade are ground out.

When the two last grades are used shorten the strokes to less than 2 in. When done the glass should be semi-transparent, and is ready for polishing.

When polishing the speculum, paste a strip of paper 1⅓ in. wide around the convex glass or tool, melt 1 lb. of pitch and turn on to it and press with the wet speculum. Mold the pitch while hot into squares of 1 in., with ¼-in. spaces, as in Fig. 1. Then warm and press again with the speculum, being careful to have all the squares touch the speculum, or it will not polish evenly. Trim the paper from the edge with a sharp knife, and paint the squares separately with jeweler's rouge, wet till soft like paint. Use a binger to spread it on with. Work the speculum over the tool the same as when grinding, using straight strokes 2 in. or less.

When the glass is polished enough to reflect some light, it should be tested with the knife-edge test. In a dark room, set the speculum against the wall, and a large lamp, L, Fig. 2, twice the focal length away. Place a large sheet of pasteboard, A, Fig. 2, with a small needle hole opposite the blaze, by the side of the lamp, so the light from the blaze will shine onto the glass. Place the speculum S, Fig. 2, so the rays from the needle hole will be thrown to the left side of the lamp (facing the speculum), with the knife mounted in a block of wood and edgeways to the lamp, as in K, Fig. 2. The knife should not be more than 6 in. from the lamp. Now move the knife across the rays from left to right, and look at the speculum with the eye on the right side of the blade. When the focus is found, if the speculum is ground and polished evenly it will darken evenly over the surface as the knife shuts off the light from the needle hole. If not, the speculum will show some dark rings, or hills. If the glass seems to have a deep

hollow in the center, shorter strokes should be used in polishing; if a hill in the center, longer strokes. The polishing and testing done, the speculum is ready to be silvered. Two glass or earthenware dishes, large enough to hold the speculum and 2 in. deep, must be procured. With pitch, cement a strip of board 8 in. long to the back of the speculum, and lay the speculum face down in one of the dishes; fill the dish with distilled water, and clean the face of the speculum with nitric acid, until the water will stick to it in an unbroken film.

The recipe for silvering the speculum is:

Solution A:
Distilled water   4 oz.
Silver nitrate   100 gr.
Solution B:
Distilled water   4 oz.
Caustic stick potash
(pure by alcohol)   100 gr.
Solution C:
Aqua Ammonia.
Solution D:
Sugar loaf   840 gr.
Nitric acid   39 gr.
Alcohol (pure)   25 gr.

Mix solution D and make up to 25 fluid oz. with distilled

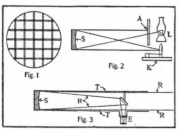

Detail of Telescope Construction

water, pour into a bottle and carefully put away in a safe place for future use, as it works better when old.

Now take solution A and set aside in a small bottle one-tenth of it, and pour the rest into the empty dish; add the ammonia solution drop by drop; a dark brown precipitate will form and subside; stop adding ammonia solution as soon as the bath clears. Then add solution B, then ammonia until bath is clear. Now add enough of the solution A, that was set aside, to bring the bath to a warm saffron color without destroying its transparency. Then add 1 oz. of solution D and stir until bath grows dark. Place the speculum, face down, in the bath and leave until the silver rises, then raise the speculum and rinse with distilled water. The small flat mirror may be silvered the same way. When dry, the silver film may be polished with a piece of chamois skin, touched with rouge, the polishing being accomplished by means of a light spiral stroke.

Fig. 3 shows the position of the glasses in the tube, also how the rays R from a star are thrown to the eyepiece E in the side of the tube. Make the tube I of sheet iron, cover with paper and cloth, then paint to make a non-conductor of heat or cold. Make the mounting of good seasoned lumber.

Thus an excellent 6-in. telescope can be made at home, with an outlay of only a few dollars. My telescope is 64 in. long and cost me just $15, but I used all my spare time in one winter in making it. I first began studying the heavens through a spyglass, but an instrument such as I desired would cost $200—more than I could afford. Then I made the one described, with which I discovered a new comet not before observed by astronomers.—John E. Mellish.

HOW TO MAKE A WATER TELESCOPE

Before you decide on a place cast your hook it is best to look into the water to sea whether any fish are there. Yes, certainly, you can look into the water and see the fish that are there

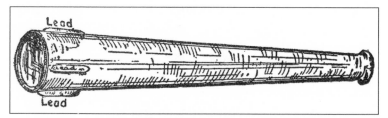

Wooden Water Telescope

swimming about, if you have the proper equipment. What you need is a water telescope. This a device made of wood or metal with one end of glass. When the glass end is submerged, by looking in at the open end, objects in the water are made plainly visible to a considerable depth. In Norway, the fishermen use the water telescope regularly in searching for herring shoals or cod.

All that is necessary to make a wooden water telescope is a long wooden box, a piece of glass for one end and some paint and putty for making the seams watertight. Fix the glass in one end of the box, and leave the other open to look through.

A tin water telescope is more convenient than the wooden one, but more difficult to make. The principle essential for this is a circular piece of glass for the large end. A funnel shaped tin horn will do for the rest. Solder in the glass at the large end and the telescope is made. Sinkers consisting of strips of lead should be soldered on near the bottom to counteract the buoyancy of the air contained in the watertight funnel and also helps to submerge the big end. The inside of the funnel should be painted black to prevent the light from being reflected on the bright surface of the tin. If difficulty is found in obtaining a circular piece of glass, the dottom may be made square and square glass used. Use plain, clear glass; not magnifying glass. To picnic parties the water telescope is of great amusement, revealing numerous odd sights in the water which many have never seen before.

How to Make a Wind Propeller

A wind propeller may be constructed with four old bicycle wheels arranged with shafts pretty much like the shafts of a hand-propelled cart. The platform is flatter, however, and the body one tier so that it is lower. A framework of wood is built at M and this is a support for several purposes. The sail is secured to the mast which is fixed into the body of the cart as shown. The sail is linen fabric. There are two crosspieces to aid in keeping the sail properly opened. The steering arrangement is through the rear shaft. The shaft is pivoted as in a hand propelled cart, and the rod I extends from the middle connection of the shaft up to a point where the person seated on the wooden

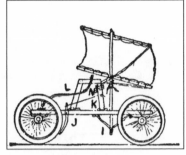

Wind Propeller

frame can handle it. There is a brake arranged by making a looped piece J and hinging it as shown. This piece is metal, fitted with a leather face. The cord K is pulled to press the brake. I marks the support for the mast underneath the body of the cart. In a steady breeze this cart spins nicely along the roads.

How to Make an Electroscope

An electroscope for detecting electrified bodies many be made out of a piece of note paper, a cork and a needle. Push the needle into the cork, and cut the paper in the shape of a small arrow. Balance the arrow on the needle as shown in the sketch, and

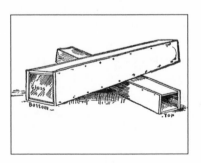

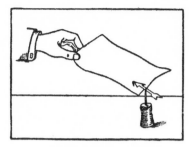

Simple Electroscope

the instrument will then be complete. If a piece of paper is then heated over a lamp or stove and rubbed with a piece of cloth or a small broom, the arrow will turn when the paper is brought near it.—Contributed by Wm. W. Grant, Halifax, N. S., Canada.

To Longer Preserve Cut Flowers

A good way to keep flowers fresh is to place a small amount of pure salt of sodium in the water. It is best to procure this salt at a drug store because commercial salt will cause the flowers to wither, due to the impurities in the soda. Call for pure sodium chloride.

Writing with Electricity

Soak piece of white paper in a solution of potassium iodide and water for about a piece of sheet metal. Connect the sheet metal with the negative or zinc side of a battery and then, using the positive wire as a pen, write your name or other inscription on the wet paper. The result will be brown lines on a white backgrounds.—Contributed by Geo. W. Fry, San Jose, Cal.

Electrolytic Writing

HOME AND LAWN FURNITURE

A BOOK REST

A book that does not open flat is rather inconvenient to write in when one of its sides is in the position shown in Fig. 2. A wedge-shaped piece of metal, stone or wood, as shown in Fig. 1, will, when placed as in Fig. 3, raise the sloping half to the level of the other pages. Cover the block with rubber, wide rubber bands or felt, to prevent its scratching the desk top. The block can also be used as a paperweight.

A BROOM HOLDER

A very simple and effective device for holding a broom when it is not in use is shown in the sketch. It is made of heavy wire and fastened to the wall with two screw-eyes, the eyes forming bearings for the wire. The small turn on the end of the straight part is to hold the hook out far enough from the wall to make it easy to place the broom in the hook. The weight of the broom keeps it in position.—Contributed by Irl Hicks, Centralia, Mo.

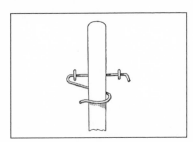

Book Back Holders

A HANGER FOR TROUSERS

Secure two clothes pins of the metal spring kind for the clamps of the hanger. The pins are fastened one to each end of a looped galvanized wire. This wire should be about 6 in. long after a coil is bent in the center as shown in the sketch. The diameter of the wire should be about ⅛ in.

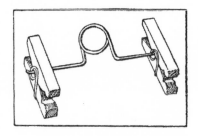

BARREL-STAVE HAMMOCK

A hammock made of barrel staves is more comfortable than one would think, considering the nature of the material employed in making it.

Good smooth staves should be selected for this purpose, and if one cares to go to a little trouble a thorough sandpapering will make a great improvement. Cut half circles out of each stave, as shown at AA, and pass ropes around the ends as shown at B. When finished the weight will then be supported by four ropes at each end, which allows the use of small-sized ropes, such as clothes lines. A hammock of this kind may be left out in the rain without injury.— Contributed by H. G. M., St. Louis, Mo.

CHILD'S FOOTREST ON AN ORDINARY CHAIR

Small chairs are enjoyed very much by children for the reason that they can rest their feet on the floor. In many households there are no small chairs for the youngsters, and

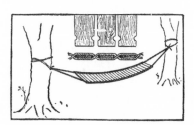

Cheap and Comfortable

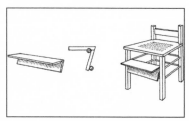

Footrest on Chair

they have to use larger ones. Two things result, the child's legs become tired from dangling unsupported or by trying to support them on the stretchers, and the finish on the chair is apt to be scratched. The device shown in the sketch forms a footrest or step that can be placed on any chair. It can be put on or taken off in a moment. Two suitable pieces of wood are nailed together at an angle and a small notch cut out, as shown, to fit the chair stretcher.

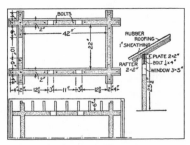

Concrete Forms

CONCRETE KENNEL

The kennel shown in the illustration is large enough for the usual size of dog. It is cleanly, healthful and more ornamental than the average kennel. This mission style would be in keeping with the now popular mission and semi-mission style home, and, with slight modifications, it could be made to conform with the ever beautiful colonial home. It is not difficult to build and will keep in good shape for many years.

The dimensions and the manner of making the forms for the concrete, and the location for the bolts to hold the plate and rafters, are shown in the diagram.—Contributed by Edith E. Lane, El Paso, Texas.

CONVENIENT SHELF ARRANGEMENT

A convenient device for crowded shelves and cupboards is shown in the accompanying sketch. Halfway between shelves A and B is installed a second shelf C which is only half as wide as the other shelves. This provides a convenient

Finished Kennel

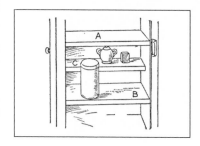

place for small articles and utensils, while in a china closet it furnishes a splendid space for cups, sauce dishes or other small pieces. It also adds a neat and pleasing appearance.— Contributed by E. M. Williams, Oberlin, Ohio.

FLOWER-POT STAND

A very useful stand for flower pots can be made of a piece of board supported by four clothes hooks. The top may be of any size suitable for the flower pot. The hooks which serve as legs are fastened to the under side of the board in the

same manner as fastening the hook to a wall.—Contributed by Oliver S. Sprout, Harrisburg, Pa.

FRAME FOR DISPLAYING BOTH SIDES OF COINS

It is quite important for coin collectors to have some convenient way to show both sides of coins without touching or handling them. If the collection consists of only a few coins, they can be arranged in frame as shown in Fig. 1. The frame is made of a heavy card, A, Fig. 2, the same thickness as the coins, and covered over on each side with a piece of glass, B. Holes are cut in the card to receive the coins C. The frame is placed on bearings so it may

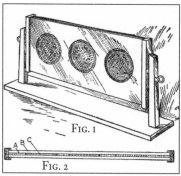

FIG. 1

FIG. 2

Holding Coins between Glasses

be turned over to examine both sides. If there is a large collection of coins, the frame can be made in the same manner and used as drawers in a cabinet. The drawers can be taken out and turned over.—Contributed by C. Purdy, Ghent, O.

HOME-MADE AQUARIUM

A good aquarium can be made from a large-sized street lamp globe and a yellow pine block. Usually a lamp globe costs less than an aquarium globe of the same dimensions. Procure a yellow pine block 3 in. thick and 12 in. square. The more uneven and twisted the grain the better for the purpose, as it is then less liable to develop a continuous crack.

Cut out a depression for the base of the globe as shown in Fig. 1. Pour in aquarium cement and embed the globe

in it. Pour more cement inside of the globe until the cement is level with the top of the block. Finish with a ring of cement around the outside and sprinkle with fine sand while the cement is damp. Feet may be added to the base if desired. The weight of the pine block makes a very solid and substantial base for the globe and renders it less liable to be upset.—Contributed by James. R. Kane, Doylestown, Pa.

Never allow lard oil to harden on a lathe.

HOMEMADE ELECTRIC STOVE

BY J. F. THOLL

The construction of an electric stove is very simple, and it can be made by any home mechanic having a vise and hand drill. The body is made of sheet or galvanized iron, cut out and drilled as shown in Fig. 1.

Each long projection represents a leg, which is bent at right angles on the center line by placing the metal in the jaws of a vise and hammering the metal over flat. If just the rim is gripped in the vise, it will give a rounding form to the lower

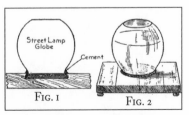

FIG. I   FIG. 2

Lamp Globe as an Aquarium

part of the legs. The small projections are bent in to form a support for the bottom.

The bottom consists of a square piece of metal, as shown in Fig. 2. Holes are drilled near the edges for stove bolts to fasten it to the bottom projections. Two of the larger holes are used for the ends of the coiled rod and the other tow for the heating-wire terminals. The latter holes should be well insulated with porcelain or mica. The top consists of a square piece of metal drilled as shown in Fig. 3. Four small ears are turned down to hold the top in place.

One end of the coiled rod is shown in Fig. 4. This illustrates how tow pins are inserted in holes, drilled at right angles, to hold the coil on the bottom plate. The coiled rod is ³⁄₁₆ in. in diameter and 27 in. long. The rod is wrapped with sheet asbestos, cut in ½-in. strips.

The length of the heating wire must be determined by the test. This wire can be purchased from electrical stores. Stovepipe wire will answer the purpose when regular heating wire cannot be obtained.

The wire is coiled around the asbestos-covered rod, so that no coil will be in contact with another coil. If, by trial, the coil does not heat sufficiently, cut some of it off and try again. About 9½ ft. of No. 26 gauge heating wire will be about right. The connection to an electric-lamp socket is made with ordinary flexible cord, to which is attached a screw plug for making connections.

GLASS-CLEANING SOLUTION

Glass tumblers, tubing and fancy bottles are hard to clean by washing them in the ordinary way, as the parts are hard to reach with the fingers or a brush. The following solution makes an excellent cleaner that will remove dirt and grease from crevices and sharp corners. To 9 parts of water add 1 part of strong parts of strong sulphuric acid. The acid should be added to the water slowly and not the water to the acid. Add as much bichromate of potash as the solution will dissolve. More bichromate of potash should be added as the precipitate is used in cleaning.

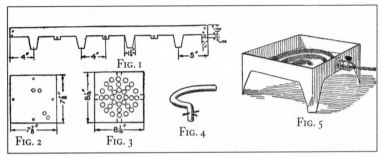

Pattern for Parts of the Electric Stove

The chemicals can be purchased cheaply from a local drug store, and made up and kept in large bottles. The solution can be used over and over and over again.—Contributed by Loren Ward, Des Moines, Iowa.

HOME-MADE NECKTIE HOLDER

The gas bracket is considered a good place to hand neckties, even if it does crowd them together. The illustration shows a better method, a curtain rod attached to one end of a bureau. Two long-shanked, square-hooked screws should be used, so they may be screwed beneath and close up to the projecting top. When removed they will leave no disfiguring

Hanger for Ties

holes.—Contributed by C. W. Neiman, New York City.

HOME-MADE OVERHEAD TROLLEY COASTER

The accompanying sketch shows a playground trolled line which furnished a great deal of amusement to many children at a minimum cost. The wire, which is $\frac{3}{16}$ in. in diameter, was stretched between a tree and

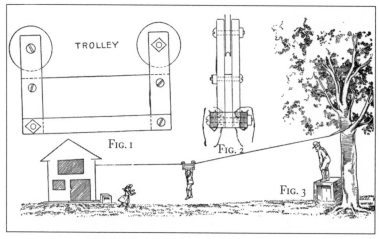

TROLLEY

FIG. I

FIG. 2

FIG. 3

Details of the Trolley and How Its Is Used

a barn across a vacant quarter block. The strength of the wire was first tested by a heavy man. When not in use the wire is unhooked from the tree and hauled into the barn and coiled loosely in the hay loft. The wire was made taut for use by a rope which was fastened to the beams in the barn. The trolley was made, as shown in Figs. 1 and 2, of strips of wood bolted with stove bolts on tow grooved pulleys. The middle wide board was made of hardwood. The wheels were taken from light pulley blocks and stove bolts were purchased from a local hardware store to accurately fit the hubs. As it was necessary

to keep the bearings greased, we used Vaseline. This coaster made great sport for the youngsters and at no time were they in danger of a serious fall as the line was hung low and the slant of the wire was moderate.—Contributed by H. J. Holden, Palm Springs, Calif.

HOMEMADE PHONOGRAPH

Make a box large enough to hold four dry cells and use it as a base to mount the motor on and to support the revolving cylinder. Anyone of the various battery motors may be used to supply the power. The support for the cylinder is first made and located on the cover of the box in such a position that it will give ample room for the motor. The motor base and the support are fastened by screws turned up through the cover or top of the box. The location of these parts is shown in Fig. 1.

The core for holding the cylindrical wax records is 4½ in. long and made of wood, turned little tapering, the diameter at the small or outer end being 1⅝ in., and at the larger end, 1⅞ in. A wood wheel with a V-shaped groove on its edge is nailed to the larger end of the cylinder. The hole in the core is fitted with a brass tube, driven in tightly to serve as a bearing. A rod that will fit the brass tube, not too tightly, but which will not wabble loose, is threaded and turned into the upper end of the support. The core with its attached driving wheel is shown in Fig. 3. The dotted lines show the brass bearing and rod axle. The end of the axle should be provided with a thread over which a washer and nut are placed, to keep the core from coming off in turning.

The sound box, Fig. 2, is about 2½ in. in diameter and

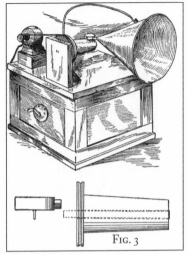

Fig. 3

Phonograph and Construction of Parts

1 in. thick, made of heavy tin. The diaphragm, which should be of thin ferrotype tin, should be soldered to the box. The needle is made of a piece of sewing needle, about ⅛ in. long, and soldered to the center of the diaphragm. The first point should be ground blunt, as shown in the sketch. When soldering these parts, together, take care to have the diaphragm lie perfectly flat and not made warping by any pressure applied while the solder is cooling.

The tin horn can be easily made, attached to the sound box

with a piece of rubber hose and held so it will swing the length of the record by a rod attached to the top of the box, as shown. The motor can be controlled by a small three or four-point battery rheostat.—Contributed by Herbert Hahn, Chicago, Ill.

HOME-MADE POST OR SWINGING LIGHT

Remove the bottom from a round bottle of sufficient size to admit a wax or tallow candle.

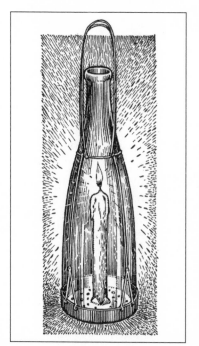

This can be done with a glass cutter or a hot ring the size of the outside of the bottle, which is slipped quickly over the end. Procure a metal can cover, a cover from a baking powder can will do, and fit it on the end where the bottom was removed. The cover is punched full of holes to admit the air and a cross cut in the center with the four wings thus made by the cutting turned up to form a place to insert the candle. The metal cover is fastened to the bottle with wires as shown in the sketch. This light can be used on a post or hung from a metal support.

HOMEMADE SHOE RACK

The accompanying sketch explains how a boy can make his own shoe rack that can be placed on the wall in the

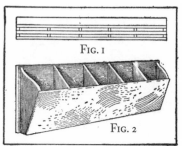

FIG. 1

FIG. 2

clothes closet. Figure 1 shows the construction of the bottom to permit the dirt to fall through. Two boards, 9 in. wide and about 3 ft. long, with six partitions between, as shown, will make pockets about 6 in. long. The width of the pockets at the bottom is 2 in. and at the top 5 in.—Contributed by Guy H. Harvey, Mill Valley, Cal.

How To Build An Imitation Street Car Line

An imitation street car line may sound like a big undertaking, but, in fact, it is one of the easiest things a boy can construct, does not take much time and the expense is not great. A boy who lives on a farm can find many fine places to run such a line, and one in town can have a line between the house and the barn, if they are some distance apart.

Often all the boards and blocks required can be had for helping a carpenter clear away the rubbish around a new building. Wheels and parts of old bicycles, which can be used in so many ways, can be found at a junk shop at very low prices, wheels in good repair are not expensive. For the car for the street car line try to find a set of wheels having axles, but if you cannot find such, make shafts of hard wood, about 3 in. by 2½ in. and by means of a jack-knife turn, or shave down the ends to receive the hub bearings of the wheels. Fasten the wheel hubs securely over the ends of the wood with pins or little bolts, or if the wheel bearing is of such a nature that it revolves

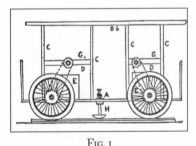

Fig. 1

Construction of Car

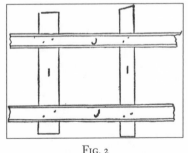

Fig. 2

Section of the Track

on its own journal, the journal can be fastened to the end of the wood piece. Each of the wheels should be provided with a sprocket; any chain sprocket of a bicycle may be used. Fasten these sprockets on the outside of the wheels as shown in Fig.1. They can be set on over the bearing end and secured with a set screw, or the original key can be employed. It is best in cases like this to use the original parts. Make the floor of the car of pieces of boards placed on the axles and nailed, screwed or bolted, as shown at A. To erect the frame, place uprights, C C C C, in position as shown, fastening the ends to the base-boards, and making the roof line as at B, then put in the crosspieces, G G. Seats, E E, are simply boxes. The drive of the car is effected by using the driving sprockets, D D,

fitted to the crosspieces, G G, with the original bearings. The parts are there by secured to the car and the chain placed on.

Key the cranks for turning to the upper sprocket's shaft and all is ready. If there are sprocket gears and cranks on either side, four boys may propel the car at one time. Considerable speed can be made on smooth roads, but it is the best amusement to run a car line on wooden tracks with a brake consisting of a piece of wooden shaft, passing through a bore in the car floor, and fitted with a leather covered pad as at H. A spiral spring holds up the brake until pressure is applied by foot power, when the brake contacts with the wooden track and checks the car.

The track plan is illustrated in Fig. 2. Get some boards and place them end for end on other pieces set as ties. The main boards on tracks, J J, can be about 6 in. wide, to the edges of which nail strips about ¾ in. wide and about the same height. The ties, I I, can be almost any box boards. Wire nails are the best to use

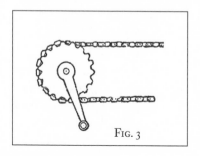

Fig. 3

in putting the tracks together. The sprocket connection with the chain is shown in Fig. 3. This consists of the sprocket gear on the propelling shaft, and the crank. The pedals may be removed and a chisel handle, or any tool handle, substituted, so as to afford means for turning the crank by hand power. Great fun can be had with the road, and, furthermore, it can be made renumerative, as boys and girls can be given rides for a penny each.

Apply a coat of raw starch water to a dirty wall before painting; this, when dry, may be brushed or wiped off.

A good varnish for electric terminals is made of sealing wax dissolved in gasoline. To prevent brittleness add a little linseed oil.

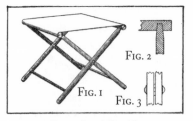

Camp Stool Details

HOW TO MAKE A CAMP STOOL

The stool, as shown in Fig. 1, is made of beech or any suitable wood with a canvas or carpet top. Provide four lengths for the legs, each 1 in. square and 18½ in. long; two lengths, 1⅛ in. square and 11 in. long, for the top, and two lengths, ¾ in. square, one 8½ and the other 10½ in. long, for the lower rails.

The legs are shaped at the ends to fit into a ⅝-in. hole bored in the top pieces as shown in Fig. 2, the distance between the centers of the holes being 7⅝ in. in one piece and 9⅝ in. in the other. The lower rails are fitted in the same way, using a ½-in. hole bored into each leg 2½ in. up from the lower end.

Each pair of legs has a joint for folding and this joint is made by boring a hole in the middle of each leg, inserting a bolt and riveting it over washers with a washer placed between the legs as shown in Fig. 3. The entire length of each part is rounded off for the sake of neatness as well as lightness.

About ½ yd. of 11-in. wide material will be required for the seat and each end of this is nailed securely on the under side of the top pieces. The woodwork may be stained and varnished or plain varnished and the cloth may be made to have a pleasing effect by stencilling in some neat pattern.

How to Make a Cup-and-Saucer Rack

The rack is made of any suitable kind of wood, and the sides, A, are cut just alike, or from one pattern. The shelves are made in various widths to fit the sides at the places where they are wanted. The number of shelves can be varied and to suit the size of the dishes. Cup hooks are placed on top and bottom shelves. It is hung on the wall the same as a picture from the molding.—Contributed by F. B. Emig, Santa Clara, Cal.

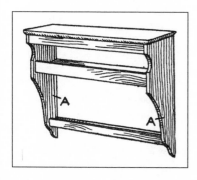

How to Make a Copper Bowl

To make a copper bowl, such as is shown in the illustration, secure a piece of No. 21 gauge sheet copper of a size sufficient to make a circular disk 6½ in. in diameter.

Cut the copper to the circular form and size just mentioned, and file the edge so that it will be smooth and free from sharp places. With a pencil compass put on a series of concentric rings about ½ in. apart. These are to aid the eye in beating the bowl to form.

The tools are simple and can be made easily. First make a round-nosed mallet of some hard wood, which should have a diameter of about 1¼ in. across the head. If nothing better is at hand, saw off a section of a broom handle, round one end and insert a handle into a hole bored in its middle. Next take a block of wood, about 3 by 3 by 6 in., and make in one end a hollow, about 2 in. across and ½ in. deep. Fasten the block solidly, as in a vise, and while holding the copper on the hollowed end of the block, beat with the mallet along the concentric rings.

Begin at the center and work along the rings—giving the copper a circular movement as the beating proceeds—out toward the rim. Continue the circular movement and work from the rim back toward the center. This operation is to be continued until the bowl has the shape desired, when the bottom is flattened by placing the bowl, bottom side up, on a flat surface and beating the raised part flat.

Beating copper tends to harden it and, if continued too long without proper treatment, will cause the metal to break. To overcome this hardness, heat the copper over a bed of coals or a Bunsen burner to a good heat. This process is called annealing, as it softens the metal.

The appearance of a bowl is greatly enhanced by the addition of a border. In the illustration the border design shown was laid out in pencil, a small hole was drilled with a band drill in each space and a small-bladed metal saw inserted and the part sawed out.

To produce color effects on copper, cover the copper with turpentine and hold over a Bunsen burner until all parts are well heated.

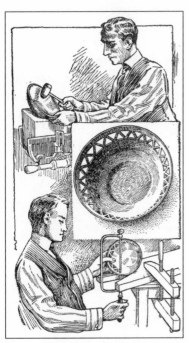

Shaping the Bowl and
Sawing the Lace

How to Make a Hammock

Any one can make a hammock as good as can be bought and that at a cost so small that every member of the family can possess one providing there are places enough for hanging them.

The materials required are a needle about 7 in. long, and with a big eye, an iron ring for each end of the hammock, two long smooth sticks on which to knit the hammock and two pounds of strong hemp cord or twine. The twine may be colored in any color or combination of colors desired. A Roman stripe at each end of the hammock makes a pretty effect.

A hammock 45 in. wide will not be too large for solid comfort. To knit it first thread the big needle and holding it in the left hand, hold the cord in place with the thumb until you have looped the cord over the tongue, then pass the cord under the needle to the opposite side and catch it over the tongue. Repeat this operation until the needle is full. Cut a 2-yd. length of cord and make a loop and fasten to the door knob or to some other convenient place. Tie the cord on the needle to this loop 3 in. from the end of the loop. Place the small mesh stick under the cord with the beveled edge close to the loop, and, with a thumb on the cord to hold it in place, pass the needle around the stick

and then, point downward, pass it through the loop from the top, and then bring it over the stick so forming the first half of the Knot.

Pull this tight and hold in place with a thumb while throwing the cord over your hand, which forms the loop. Pass the needle from under through the loops and draw fast to fasten the knot. Hold this in place and repeat the operation.

Make 30 of these knots and then push them off the stick and proceed in the same way with the next row, passing the needle first through each of the 30 knots made for the first row. Make 30 rows and then tie the last loops to the other iron ring. Stretchers may be made and put in place and the hammock, strong and durable, is finished. The work must be carefully and evenly done. One is apt to have a little trouble getting the first row right, but after that the work proceeds quite rapidly.

HOW TO MAKE A MINIATURE STAGE

A good smooth box, say 8 in. wide, 10 in. high and 12 in.

Fig. 1 FIGURES ON TAPE Fig. 3 Fig. 2

Details of the Miniature Mechanical Stage

long, will serve the purpose for the main part of this small theater. Cut two rectangular holes, Fig. 1, one in each end and exactly opposite each other. Place a screw eye about ½ in. from the edge on each side of these openings. Fit an axle in the screw eyes and fasten a spool to the middle of the axle. On one of the two spools attach another smaller spool, Fig. 2, to be used as a driving pulley. Cut out the front part of the box down to a level with the top of the spools.

Connect the spools with a belt made from tape about ¾ in. wide. On this belt fasten figures cut from heavy paper and made in the form of people, automobiles, trolley cars, horses and dogs. A painted scenery can be made in behind the movable tape. The front part

of the box may be draped with curtains, making the appearance of the ordinary stage, as shown in Fig. 3. A small motor will run the spools and drive the tape on which the figures are attached.—Contributed by William M. Crilly, Jr., Chicago.

HOW TO MAKE A PHONOGRAPH RECORD CABINET

The core, Fig. 1, consists of six strips of wood beveled so as to form six equal sides. The strips are 3 ft. long and 3 in. wide on the outside bevel and are nailed to three blocks made hexagon, as shown in Fig. 2, from ⅞-in. material. One block is placed at each end and one in the middle. A ½-in. metal pin is driven in a hole bored in the center of each end block. The bottoms of the pasteboard cases, used to hold the wax records, are either tacked or glued to this hexagon core, as shown in Fig. 3, with their open ends outward.

Two circular pieces are made of such a diameter as will cover the width of the core and the cases attached, and extend about ½ in. each side. A ½-in. hole is bored in the center of these pieces to receive the pins placed in the ends of the core, Fig. 1. These will form the ends of the cabinet, and when placed, one on each end of the core, heavy building paper or sheet metal is tacked around them for a covering, as shown in Fig. 4. A small glass door is made, a little wide r than one row of cases, and fitted in one side of the covering. The outside may be painted or decorated in any way to suit the builder.

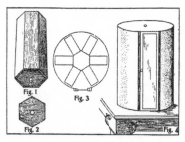

Phonograph Wax Record Case

How To Make A Porch Swing Chair

The material needed for making this porch swing chair are two pieces of round wood 2½ in. in diameter and 20 in. long, and two pieces 1¼ in. in diameter and 40 in. long. These longer pieces can be made square, but for appearance it is best to have them round or square with the corners rounded. A piece of canvas, or other stout cloth, 16 in. wide and 50 in. long, is to be used for the seat. The two short pieces of wood are used for the ends of the chair and two 1-in. holes are bored in each end of them 1½ in. from the ends, and between the holes and the ends grooves are cut around them to make a place to fasten ropes, as shown at B, Fig. 1. The two longer pieces are used for the sides and a tenon is cut on each end of them to fit in the 1-in. holes bored in the end pieces, as shown at A, Fig. 1. The canvas is now tacked on the end pieces and the pieces given one turn before placing the mortising together.

The chair is now hung up to the porch ceiling with ropes attached to a large screw eye or

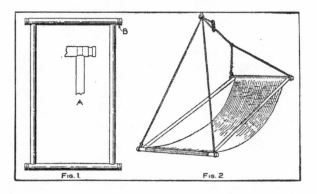

Fig. 1.   Fig. 2

hook. The end of the chair to be used for the lower part is held about 16 in. from the floor with ropes direct from the grooves in the end pieces to the hook. The upper end is supported by using a rope in the form of a loop or bail, as shown in Fig. 2. The middle of the loop or bail should be about 15 in. from the end piece of the chair. Another rope is attached to the loop and through the hook and to a slide as shown. This will allow for adjustment to make the device into a chair or a hammock.—Contributed by Earl R. Hastings, Corinth, Vt.

HOW TO MAKE A POST CARD HOLDER

This holder is designed to lay flat on the counter or to stack one on top of the other, keeping each variety of cards separate, or a number of their can be fastened on any upright surface to display either horizontal or vertical cards.

The holder can be made from sheet tin, zinc, brass or aluminum. The dimensions for the right size are given in Fig. 1; the dotted line showing where the bends are made. The completed holder is

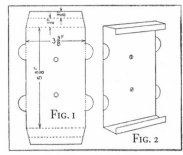

Fig. 1   Fig. 2

Pattern for Cutting the Metal

shown in Fig. 2 as fastened to a wall.—Contributed by John F. Williamson, Daytona, Fla.

Do not allow paint that is left over from a job to stand uncovered. The can should be tightly sealed and the paint will be found suitable for use foi several days.

How to Make a Sconce

A sconce is a candlestick holder, so made that it has a reflector of brass or copper and is to hang upon the wall. The tools necessary are a riveting hammer, file, metal shears, rivet punch, flat and round-nosed pliers, screwdriver and sheet brass or copper No. 23 gauge.

To make the sconce proceed as follows: First, cut off a piece of brass so that it shall have ½ in. extra metal all around; second, with a piece of carbon paper, trace upon the brass lines that shall represent the margin of the sconce proper, also trace the decorative design; third, with a nailset make a series of holes in the extra margin about ¾ in. apart and large enough to take in a ¾-in. thin screw; fourth, fasten the metal to a thick board by inserting screws in these holes; fifth, with a twenty-penny wire nail that has had the sharpness of its point filed off, stamp the background of the design promiscuously. By holding the nail about ¼ in. above the work and striking it with the hammer, at the same time striving to keep its point at ¼ in. above the metal, very rapid progress can be made. This stamping lowers the background and at the same time raises the design. Sixth, chase or stamp along the border of the

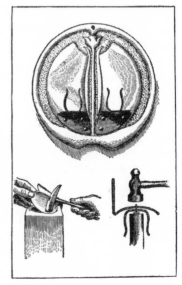

Completed Sconce

Shaping the Holders   Riveting

design and background using a nail filed to a chisel edge. This is to make a clean sharp division between background and design. Seventh, when the stamping is complete remove the screws and metal from the board and cut off the extra margin with the metal shears. File the edges until they are smooth to the touch.

The drip cup is a piece of brass cut circular and shaped by placing the brass over a hollow in one end of a block. Give the metal a circular motion, at the same time beat it with a round-nosed mallet. Work from the center along concentric rings outward, then reverse.

The candle holders may have two, three, four, six arms, and are bent to shape by means of the round-nosed pliers. The form of the brackets which support the drip cups may be seen in the illustration.

Having pierced the bracket, drip cup, and holder, these three parts are riveted together as indicated in the drawing. It will be found easier usually if the holder is not shaped until after the riveting is done. The bracket is then riveted to the back of the sconce. Small copper rivets are used.

It is better to polish all the pieces before fastening any of them together. Metal polish of any kind will do. After the parts have been assembled a lacquer may be applied to keep the metal from tarnishing.

HOW TO MAKE AN AQUARIUM

In making an aquarium, the first thing to decide on is the size. It is well not to attempt building a very large one, as the difficulties increase with the size. A good size is 12 by 12 by 20 in., and this is inexpensive to build.

First buy one length of ¾ by ⅛-in. angle iron for the frame, F, Fig. 1. This can be obtained at any steel shop and should cost about 20 cents. All the horizontal pieces, B, should be beveled 45°. at the ends and drilled for ³⁄₁₆-in. stove bolts. The beveling may be done by roughing out with a hacksaw and finishing with a file. After all the pieces are cut and beveled they should be drilled at the ends for the ³⁄₁₆-in. stove bolts, C. Drill all the horizontal pieces, B, first

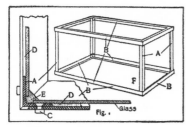

Detail of Aquarium Frame

and then mark the holes on the upright pieces, A, through the holes already drilled, thus making all the holes coincide. Mark the ends of each piece with a figure or letter, so that when they are assembled, the same ends will come together again. The upright pieces, A, should be countersunk as shown in the detail, and then the frame is ready to assemble.

After the frame has been assembled take it to glazier and have a bottom made of skylight glass, and sides and ends of double-thick window glass. The bottom glass should be a good fit, but the sides and ends should be made slightly shorter to allow the cement, E, to form a dovetail joint as shown. When the glass is put in the frame a space, D, will be found between the glass and the horizontal

pieces, B, of the frame. If this were allowed to remain the pressure of the water would spring the glass and cause a leak at E; so it is filled up with plaster of paris.

The cement, E, is made as follows: Take 1 gill of plaster of paris, 1 gill of litharge, 1 gill of fine white sand, and ⅓ of a gill of finely powdered rosin. Mix well and add boiled linseed oil and turpentine until as thick as putty. Let the cement dry three or four days before putting any water in the aquarium.

In choosing stock for the aquarium it should be remembered that a sufficient quantity of vegetable life is required to

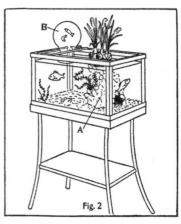

Aquarium Finished

furnish oxygen for the fish. In a well balanced aquarium the water requires renewal only two or three times a year. It is well to have an excess of plants and a number of snails, as the snails will devour all the decaying vegetable matter which would otherwise poison the water and kill the fish.

If desired, a centerpiece (A, Fig. 2) can be made of colored stones held together by cement, and an inverted jar can be supported in the position shown at B. If the mouth of the jar is below the surface of the water it will stay filled and allow the fish to swim up inside as shown. Some washed pebbles or gravel should be placed on the bottom, and, if desired, a few Chinese lilies or other plants may be placed on the centerpiece.

HOW TO MAKE AN EASEL

A strong and substantial easel may be made at home with very little expense and no great difficulty.

Smooth down with a plane, four piece of pine, 1 in. thick, 4 in. wide and 4 ft. long, until suitable for legs. Make three cross-pieces, Fig. 1, and join the legs with them as shown in Fig. 2. With an auger bore a hole in each leg about 3 in. from the bottom, and fit into each a little peg, Fig. 2, for the picture to rest on. The peg should be of hardwood so it will not break.

Cut the handle from an old broom, measure off the right length, and put a hinge on one end. Fasten this leg on the second cross-piece, thus forming a support for the two front legs, Fig. 3. The easel

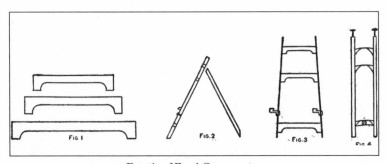

Details of Easel Construction

may be finished according to the individuals taste. It may be sand-papered and stained and varnished, or painted in some pretty tint, or, if preferred, may be enameled.—Contributed by G. J. Tress.

HOW TO MAKE AN INEXPENSIVE WOODEN FAN

Select a nice straight-grained piece of white pine about 1⁄4 in. thick, ¾ in. wide and 4 in. long. Lay out the design desired and cut as shown in Fig. 1, and then soak the wood in hot water to make it soft and easy to split. Cut the divisions very thin with a sharp knife down to the point A, as shown in the sketch, taking care not to split the wood through the part left for the handle. The fan is then finished by placing each

piece over the other as in Fig. 2. This will make a very pretty ornament.—Contributed by Fred W. Whitehouse, Upper Troy, N. Y.

QUICKLY MADE LAWN TENT

A very simple way of erecting a lawn tent for the children is to take a large umbrella such as used on delivery wagons and drive the handle into the ground deep enough to hold it solid. Fasten canvas or cotton cloth to the ends of the ribs and let it hang so that the bottom edge will touch the ground. Light ropes can be tied to the ends of the ribs and fastened to stakes driven in the ground in a tent-like manner to make the whole more substantial and to

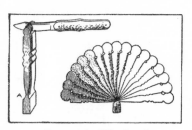

Cutting the Wood and
Complete Fan

Lawn Tent Complete

stand against a heavy wind. This makes an exceptionally fine tent, as the umbrella is waterproof; also, there is more room to stand up in than in a tent that is in the shape of a wigwam.—Contributed by J. A. Whamer, Schenectady, N. Y.

RUBBER TIP FOR CHAIR LEGS

An inexpensive method of preventing a chair from scratching the floor is to bore a hole of the proper size in the bottom end of each chair leg and then procure four rubber stoppers of uniform size and press them into place.

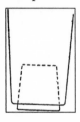

This cushion of rubber eliminates vibrations and they will not slip nor mar the finest surface upon which they rest.—Contributed by W. A. Jaquythe, Richmond, Cal.

RUSTIC WINDOW BOXES

Instead of using an ordinary green-painted window box, why not make an artistic one in which the color does not clash with the plants contained in it but rather harmonizes with them.

Such a window box can be made by anyone having usual mechanical ability, and will furnish more opportunities for artistic and original design than many other articles of more complicated construction.

The box proper should be made a little shorter than the length of the window to allow for the extra space taken up in trimming and should be nearly equal in width to the sill, as shown in Fig. 1. If the sill is inclined, as is usually the case, the box will require a greater height in front, to make it set level, as shown in Fig. 2.

The box should be well nailed or screwed together and should then be painted all over to make it more durable. A number of ½-in. holes should be drilled in the bottom, to allow the excess water to run out and thus prevent rotting of the plants and box.

Having completed the bare box, it may be trimmed to suit the fancy of the maker. The design shown in Fig. 1 is very simple and easy to construct,

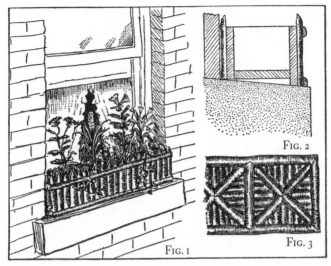

FIG. 2

FIG. 1

FIG. 3

Artistic Flower Boxes

but may be replaced with a panel or other design. One form of panel design is shown in Fig. 3.

Trimming having too rough a surface will be found unsuitable for this work as it is difficult to fasten and cannot be split as well as smooth trimming. It should be cut the proper length before being split and should be fastened with brads. The half-round hoops of barrels will be found very useful in trimming, especially for filling-in purposes, and by using them the operation of splitting is avoided. After the box is trimmed, the rustic work should be varnished, in order to thoroughly preserve it, as well as improve its appearance.

ANTIDOTE FOR SQUIRREL PEST

To the owner of a garden in a town where squirrels are protected by law, life in the summer time is a vexation. First the squirrels dig up the sweet corn and two or three replantings are necessary. When the corn is within two or three days of being suitable for cooking, the squirrels come in droves from far and near. They eat all they can and carry away the rest. When the corn is gone cucumbers, cabbages, etc., share the same fate, being partly eaten into. At the risk of being arrested for killing the squirrels I have used a small target rifle morning and night, but during my absence the devastation went on steadily. Last year they destroyed my entire corn crop. Traps do no good; can't use poison, too dangerous. But I have solved the difficulty; it's easy.

Shake cayenne pepper over the various vegetables which are being ruined, and observe results.

Self-Lighting Arc Searchlight

A practical and easily constructed self-lighting arc searchlight can be made in the following manner: Procure a large, about 6 in. in diameter, and cut three holes in its side about 2 in. from the back end, and in the positions shown in the sketch. Two of the holes are cut large enough to hold a short section of a garden hose

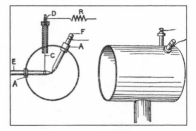

Arc in Large Tin can

tightly, as shown at AA. A piece of porcelain tube, B, used for insulation, is fitted tightly in the third hole. The hose insulation A should hold the carbon F rigidly, while the carbon E should rest loosely in its insulation.

The inner end of the carbon E is supported by a piece of No. 25 German-silver wire, C, which is about 6 in. long. This wire runs through the porcelain tube to the binding post D. The binding post is fastened to a wood plug in the end of the tube. The tube B is adjusted so that the end of the carbon E is pressing against the carbon F. The electric wires are connected to the carbon F and the binding post D. A resistance, R, should be in the line.

The current, in passing through the lamp, heats the

strip of German-silver wire, causing it to expand. This expansion lowers the end of the carbon E, separating the points of the two carbons and thus providing a space between them for the formation of an arc. When the current is turned off, the German-silver wire contracts and draws the two carbon ends together ready for lighting again. The feed can be adjusted by sliding the carbon F through its insulation.

A resistance for the arc may be made by running the current through a water rheostat or through 15 ft. of No. 25 gauge German-silver wire.— Contributed by R. H. Galbreath, Denver, Colo.

SAFETY TIPS ON CHAIR ROCKERS

Some rocking chairs are so constructed that when the person occupying it gives a hard tilt backward, the chair tips over or dangerously near it. A rubber-tipped screw turned into the under side of each rocker, near the rear end, will prevent the chair from tipping too for back.

TIGHTENING CANE IN FURNITURE

Split cane, used as part of furniture, such as chair seats, often becomes loose and the threads of cane pull out. This can be prevented by sponging with hot water, or by applying steaming cloths to the cane. This process also tightens the shreds of cane and does not injure ordinary furniture. If the article is highly polished, care should be taken to prevent the hot water from coming in contact with anything but the cane.

TURN-DOWN SHELF FOR A SMALL SPACE

The average amateur photographer does not have very much space in which to do his work. The kitchen is the room used ordinarily for finishing the photographs. In many instances

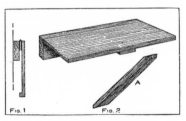

Turn-Down Shelf

there will not be space enough for any extra tables, and so a temporary place is prepared from boxes or a chair on which to place the trays and chemicals. Should there be space enough on one of the walls a shelf can be made to hang down out of the way when not in use. A shelf constructed on this order may be of any length to suit the space or of such a length for the purpose intended. A heavy piece of wood, about 1½ in. thick, and 4 to 6 in. wide, is first fastened to the wall at the proper height with nails, or, much better, large screws.

The shelf is cut and planed smooth from a board 12 in. wide and about 1 in. thick. This board is fastened to the piece on the wall with two hinges as shown in Fig. 1. A small cleat is nailed to the outer and under edge of the board and in the middle as shown. This is used to place a support under the outer edge of the shelf. The support, A, Fig. 2, should be long enough to extend diagonally to the floor or top of the baseboard from the inner edge of the cleat when the shelf is up in its proper place.—L. L.

HOME-MADE TOOLS

A FISHHOOK BOX

A box that may be used to hold fishhooks, sinkers, matches or any small articles, can be made from two empty shot-gun cartridges as shown in the sketch. The paper is cut from the brass part of one shell at the place marked A, Fig. 1, and the brass part, Fig 2, is used for a cap on the other shell (Fig. 3). Coating the box with shellac will improve its

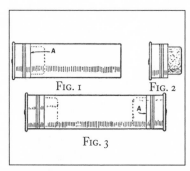

Made of Shotgun Shells

appearance.—Contributed by Abner B. Shaw, N. Dartmouth, Mass.

A HANDY CALENDAR

"Thirty days hath September, April, June and November," etc., and many other rhymes and devices are used to aid the memory to decide how many days are in each month of the year. Herewith is illustrated a very simple method to determine the number of days in any month. Place the first finger of your right hand on the first knuckle of your left hand, calling that knuckle January; then drop your finger into the depression between the first and second knuckles, calling this February; then the second knuckle will be March, and so on, until you reach July on

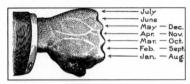

The knuckles Designate the 31-Day Months

the knuckle of the little finger, then begin over again with August on the first knuckle and continue until December is reached. Each month as it falls upon a knuckle will have 31 days and those down between the knuckles 30 days with the exception of February which has only 28 days.—Contributed by Chas. C. Bradley, West Toledo, Ohio.

A HOME-MADE FLOOR POLISHER

An inexpensive floor polisher can be made as follows: Secure a wooden box with a base 8 by 12 in. and about 6 in. high, also piece of new carpet, 14 by 18 in. Cut 3-in. squares out of the four corners of the carpet and place the box squarely on it. Turn three of the flaps of the carpet up and tack them securely to the sides of the box. Before tacking the fourth side,

fold a couple of newspapers to the right size and shove them in between the carpet and the bottom of the box for a cushion. Fill the box with any handy ballast, making it heavy or light, according to who is going to use it, and securely nail on the top of the box. The handle can be made from an old broom handle the whole of which will be none too long. Drive a heavy screweye into the big end of the handle and fasten to the polisher by a staple driven through the eye into the center of the cover, thus making a universal joint. The size of the box given here is the best although any size near that, if not too high, will answer the purpose just as well. The box is pushed or pulled over the floor and the padded side will produce a fine polish.

A HOME-MADE HAND VISE

A very useful little hand vise can easily be made from a hinge and a bolt carrying a wing nut. Get a fast joint hinge about 2 in. or more long and a bolt about ½ in. long that will fit the holes in the hinge. Put the bolt through the middle hole of the hinge and replace the nut as shown in the drawing. With this device any small abject may be firmly held by simply placing it between the sides of the hinge and tightening the nut.

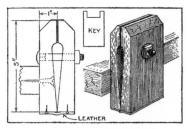

Details of a Home-Made Bench Vise

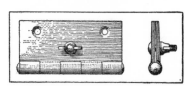

Hand Vise Made from a Hinge

A HOME-MADE VICE

Cut two pieces of wood in the shape shown in the sketch and bore a ⅜-in. hole through both of them for a common carriage bolt. Fasten one of the pieces to the edge of the bench with a large wood screw and attach the other piece to the first one with a piece of leather nailed across the bottom of both pieces. The nut on the carriage bolt may be tightened with a wrench, or better still, a key filed out of a piece of soft steel to fit the nut. The edges of the jaws are faced with sheet metal which can be copper or steel suitable for the work it is intended to hold.

A HOME-MADE VISE

While making a box I had some dovetailing to do, and as there was no vise on the bench I rigged up a substitute. I secured a board ¾ in. thick, 3 in. wide and 20 in. long and bored a ½-in. hole through it, 1 in. from each end. The board was then attached to the bench with two screws passing through washers and the two holes in the board into the bench top. The screws should be of a length suitable to take in the piece to be

Vise on Bench

worked.—Contributed by A. M. Rice, Syracuse, New York.

A Homemade Water Motor

BY MRS. PAUL S. WINTER

In these days of modern improvements, most houses are equipped with a washing-machine, and the question that arises in the mind of the house-holder is how to furnish the power to run it economically. I referred this question to my husband, with the result that he built a motor which proved so very satisfactory that I prevailed upon him to give the readers of Amateur Mechanics a descrip-tion of it, hoping it may solve the same question for them.

A motor of this type will develop about ½ hp. With a water pressure of 70 lb. The power developed is correspond-ingly increased or decreased as the pressure exceeds or falls below this. In the latter case the power may be increased by using a smaller pulley. Fig. 1 is the motor with one side removed, showing the paddle-wheel in position; Fig. 2 is an end view; Fig. 3 shows one of the paddles, and Fig. 4 shows the method of shaping the paddles. To make the frame, several lengths of scantling 3 in. wide by 1 in. thick (prefer-ably of hard wood) are required. Cut two of them 4 ft. long, to form the main supports of the frame, AA, Fig. 1; another, 2 ft. 6 in. long, for the top, B, Fig. 1; another, 26 in. long, to form the slanting part, C, Fig. 1; and another, D, approximately 1 ft., according to the slant given C. After nailing these together as shown in the illustration, nail two short strips on each side of the outlet, as at E, to keep the frame from spreading.

Cut two pieces 30 in. long. Lay these on the sides of the frame with their center lines along the line FF, which is 15 in. from the outside top of the frame. They are shown in fig. 2 at GG. Do not fasten these boards now, but mark their position on the frame. Two short boards 1 in. wide by 1 in. thick (HH, Fig. 2) and another 1 in. by 1½ in. (I, Fig. 2) form a substantial base.

Cut the wheel from sheet iron ¹⁄₁₆ in. thick, 24 in. in diam-eter. This can be done roughly with hammer and chisel and

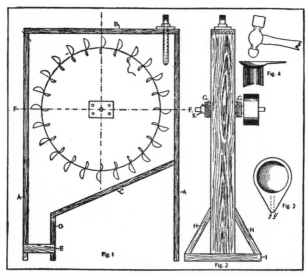

Detail of Homemade Waterwheel

then smoothed up on an emery wheel, after which cut 24 radial slots ¾ in. deep on its circumference by means of a hacksaw. On each side of the wheel at the center fasten a rectangular piece of ¼-in. iron 3 by 4 in. and secure it to the wheel by means of four rivets; after which drill a ⅝-in. hole through the exact center of the wheel.

Cut 24 pieces of ⅟₃₂-in. iron, 1½ by 2½ in. These are the paddles. Shape them by placing one end over a section of 1-in. pipe, and hammer bowl-shaped with the peen of a hammer, as shown in Fig. 4. Then cut them into the shape shown in Fig. 3 and bend the tapered end in along the lines JJ, after which place them in the slots of the wheel and bend the sides over to clamp the wheel. Drill ⅛-in. holes through the wheel and sides of the paddles and rivet paddles in place. Next secure a ⅝-in. steel shaft 12 in. long to the wheel about 8 in. from one end by means of a key. This is done by cutting a groove in the shaft and a corresponding groove in the wheel and fitting in a piece of metal in order to secure the wheel from turning independently of the shaft. Procure two collars or round pieces of brass (KK, Fig. 2) with a ⅝-in. hole through them, and fasten these to the shaft by means of set screws to prevent it from moving lengthwise.

Make the nozzle by taking a piece of ½-in. galvanized pipe 3½ in. long and filling it with babbitt metal; then drill a ³⁄₁₆-in. hole through its center. Make this hole conical, tapering from ³⁄₁₆ in. to a full ½ in. This is best done by using a square taper reamer. Then place the nozzle in the position shown in Fig. 1, which allows the stream of water to strike the buckets full in the center when they reach the position farthest to the right.

Take the side pieces, GG, and drill a 1-in. hole through their sides centrally, and a ¼-in. hole from the tops to the 1-in. holes. Fasten them in their proper position, with the wheel and shaft in place, the shaft projecting through the holes just mentioned. Now block the wheel; that is, fasten it by means of wedges or blocks of wood until the shaft is exactly in the center of the inch holes in the side pieces. Cut four disks of cardboard to slip over the shaft and large enough to cover the inch holes. Two of these are to be inside and two outside of the frames (one to bear against each side of each crosspiece). Fasten these to the crosspieces by means of tacks to hold them securely. Pour melted babbitt metal into the ¼-in. hole to form the bearings. When it has cooled, remove the cardboard, take down the crosspieces, and drill a ⅛-in. hole from the top of the crosspieces through the babbitt for an oil-hole.

Secure sufficient sheet zinc to cover the sides of the frame. Cut the zinc to the same shape as the frame and let it extend down to the crosspieces EE. Tack one side on. (It is well to tack strips of heavy cloth—burlap will do—along the edges under the zinc to form a water-tight joint.) Fasten the crosspiece over the zinc in its proper position. Drill a hole through the zinc, using the hole in the crosspiece as a guide. Then put the wheel in a central position in the frame, tack the other side piece of zinc in place and put the other crosspiece in place. Place the two collars mentioned before on the shaft, and fasten so as to bear against the crosspieces, in order to prevent the wheel and shaft from moving sidewise. If the bearings are now oiled, the shaft should turn easily and smoothly. Fasten a pulley 4 or 6 in. in diameter to the longest arm of the shaft.

Connect the nozzle to a water faucet by means of a piece of hose; place the outlet over a drain, and belt the motor direct to the washing-machine, sewing-machine, ice-cream freezer, drill press, dynamo or any other machinery requiring not more than ½ hp.

This motor has been in use in our house for two years in all of the above ways, and has never once failed to give perfect satisfaction. It is obvious that, had the wheel and paddles been made of brass, it would be more durable, but as it would have cost several times as much, it is a question whether it would be more economical in the end. If sheet-iron is used, a coat of heavy paint would prevent rust and therefore prolong the life of the motor. The motor will soon pay for itself in the saving of laundry bills. We used to spend $1 a month to have just my husband's overalls done at the laundry, but now I put them in the machine, start the motor, and leave them for an hour or so. At the end of this time they are perfectly clean, and I have noticed that they wear twice as long as when I sent them to the laundry.

A Temporary Funnel

The amateur photographer often has some solution which he desires to put into a bottle which his glass funnel will not fit, says the Photographic Times. The funnel made by rolling up a piece of paper usually allows half of the solution to run down the outside of the bottle, thereby causing the amateur to be dubbed a "musser." A better way is to take an ordinary envelope and cut it off as shown

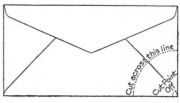

Paper Funnel

by the dotted lines. Then clip a little off the point, open out, and you have a funnel that will not give any trouble. It is cheap and you can afford to throw it away when dirty, thereby saving time and washing.

A Shot Scoop

In the ammunition department of our hardware store the shot was kept in regular square

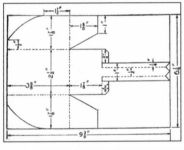

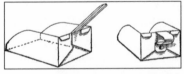

A Small Square Scoop Made of Tin for Dipping Up Shot Stored in a Square Bin

bins and dished out with a round-bottom scoop. This was very difficult, especially when the bottom of the bin was

nearly reached, as the round scoop would roll over them and only pick up a few at a time. To overcome this difficulty I constructed a square-shaped scoop that gave entire satisfaction. The scoop can be used for other purposes as well.

A thick piece of tin, 6 ¼ by 9 ¾ in., was marked out as shown, the pattern being cut on the full lines and bent on the dotted ones. The strip for the handle was riveted to the end of the scoop.—Contributed by Geo. B. Wright, Middletown, Conn.

A Tool for Lifting Can Covers

A handy tool for prying up varnish, paint, syrup and similar can covers can be made from and old fork filed down to the shape shown in the illustration. The end is filed to an edge, but not sharp.—Contributed by Ben Grebin, Ashland, Wis.

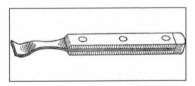

Made of an Old Fork

An Automatic Lock

The illustration shows an automatic lock operated by electricity, one cell being sufficient. When the circuit is broken a weight, A, attached to the end of the armature B, tends to push the other end of the armature into the screw eye or hook C, which is in the door, thus locking the door.

To unlock the door, merely push the button E. The magnet then draws the armature out of the screw eye and the door is unlocked. The dotted line at D shows the position of the armature when the circuit is complete and the door unlocked. The weight must be in proportion to the strength of the magnet. If it is not, the door will not lock, or would remain locked. The button can be hidden, as it is the key to the lock.—Contributed by Claude B. Melchior, Hutchinson, Minn.

An Egg-Shell Funnel

Bottles having small necks are hard to fill without spilling the liquid. A funnel cannot be used in a small opening, and pouring with a graduate glass requires a steady hand. When you do not have a graduate at hand, a half egg-shell with a small hole pricked in the end will serve better than a funnel. Place the shell in an oven to brown the surface slightly and it will be less brittle and last much longer.—Contributed by Maurice Baudier, New Orleans, La.

Cleaner for White Shoes

Finely ground whiting mixed with water to the consistency of paste makes a very good coating for white shoes. A brush can be used in applying the mixture which will dry in a few minutes. It is best to mix only as much paste as required for immediate use.—Contributed by L. Szerlip, Brooklyn, N. Y.

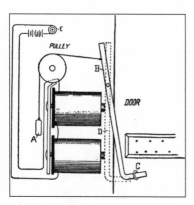

Automatic Electric Lock for Doors

CLEANING LEATHER ON FURNITURE

Beat up the whites of three eggs carefully and use a piece of flannel to rub it well into the leather which will become clean and lustrous. For black leathers, some lampblack may be added and the mixture applied in the same way.

COUNTER BRUSH FOR A SHOP

A very serviceable brush for use around a shop can be made from a discarded or worn-out push broom as shown at A. Pull out the bristles from one-half of the brush and shape the wood of that end with a knife or spoke-shave to the form of a handle, and the brush will be formed as shown at B.—Contributed by James T. Gaffney, Chicago.

A Discarded Push Broom Shaped to Form a Brush for the Bench or Counter

CRUTCH MADE OF AN OLD BROOM

An emergency crutch made of a worn-out broom is an excellent substitute for a wood crutch, especially when one or more crutches are needed for a short time, as in cases of a sprained ankle, temporary lameness, or a hip that has been wrenched.

Shorten and hollow out the brush of the broom and then pad the hollow part with cotton batting, covering it with a piece of

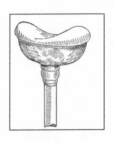

cloth sewed in place. Such a crutch does not heat the arm pit and there is an elasticity about it not to be had in the wooden crutch. The crutch can be made to fit either child or adult, and, owing to its cheapness, can be thrown away when no longer needed.—Contributed by Katharine D. Morse, Syracuse, N. Y.

ELECTRIC DOOR-OPENER

A very convenient and efficient device for unlocking any door fitted with a spring lock is shown in the accompanying sketches. A fairly stiff spring,

A, is connected by a flexible wire cord to the knob B. The cord is also fastened to a lever, C, which is pivoted at D and is released by a magnetic trigger, E, made from the armature and magnet of an old electric bell.

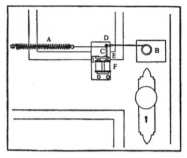

Apparatus Placed on Inside of Door

When the circuit is completed by means of a secret contact device outside the door, the magnet, F, pulls down the armature, which releases the trigger and allows the spring to open the lock. If there are metal numbers on the outside of the door they may be used for the secret contact, if desired, but if there are no numbers on the door, a small contact-board may be constructed by driving about 12 brass-headed tacks into a thin piece of wood and making connections at the back as shown in the wiring diagram.

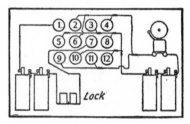

Wiring Diagram

In this particular diagram the tacks numbered 1 and 7 are used for unlocking the door, the others being connected with the electric-bell circuit as indicated, for the purpose of giving an alarm should anybody try to experiment with the secret contacts. By means of a pocket knife or other metal article the operator can let himself in at any time by connecting the tacks numbered 1 and 7, while a person not knowing the combination would be liable to sound the alarm. Of course, the builder of this device may choose a combination of his own and may thus prevent anybody else from entering the door, even those who read this description.—Contributed by Perry A. Borden, Gachville, N. B.

HOMEMADE FLOOR POLISHER

A floor polisher is something that one does not use

but two or three times a year. Manufactured polishers come in two sizes, one weighing 15 lb., which is the right weight for family use, and one weighing 25 lb.

A polisher can be made at home that will do the work just as well. Procure a wooden box such as cocoa tins or starch packages are shipped in and stretch several thicknesses of flannel or carpet over the bottom, allowing the edges to extend well up the sides, and tack smoothly. Make handle of two stout strips of wood, 36 in. long, by joining their upper ends to a shorter crosspiece and nail it to the box. Place three paving bricks inside of the box, and the polisher will weigh about 16 lb., just the right weight for a woman to use. The polisher is used by rubbing with the grain of the wood.— Contributed by Katharine D. Morse, Syracuse, N.Y.

HOME-MADE LANTERN

The accompanying picture shows a lantern which can be made almost anywhere for immediate use. All that is needed, is an empty tomato or coffee can, a piece of wire and a candle. Make a hole a little smaller than the diameter of a candle and about one-third of the way from the closed end of the can, as shown. A wire is tied around the can, forming a handle for carrying. This kind of lantern can be carried against almost any wind and the light will not be blown out.—Contributed by G. A. Sloan, Duluth, Minn.

Tin Can Lantern

HOMEMADE SCROLL SAW

A scroll saw, if once used, becomes indispensable in any home carpenter chest, yet it is safe to say that not one in ten contains it. A scroll saw is much more useful than a key-hole saw for sawing small and irregular holes, and many fancy knick-knacks, such as brackets, bookracks and shelves can be made with one.

A simple yet serviceable scroll saw frame can be made from a piece of cold-rolled steel rod, $\frac{3}{32}$ or ¼ in. in diameter, two ⅛-in. machine screws, four washers and four square nuts. The rod should be 36 or 38 in. long, bent as shown in Fig. 1. Place one washer on each screw and put the screws through the eyelets, A A, then place other washers on and fasten in place by screwing one nut on each screw, clamping the washers against the frame as tightly as possible. The saw, which can be purchased at a local hardware store, is fastened between the clamping nut and another nut as shown in Fig. 2.

If two wing nuts having the same number and size of threads are available, use them in place of the outside nuts. They are easier to turn when inserting a saw blade in a hole or when removing broken blades.—Contributed by W. A. Scranton, Detroit, Michigan.

HOW TO MAKE A CANOE

A practical and serviceable canoe, one that is inexpensive, can be built by any boy, who can wield hammer and saw, by closely following the instructions and drawings, given in this article.

It is well to study these carefully before beginning the actual work. Thus an understanding will be gained of how the parts fit together, and of the way to proceed with the work.

Dimensioned drawings of the canoe and molds are contained in Fig. 1. The boat is built on a temporary base, A, Fig. 2, which is a board, 14 ft. 1 in. long, 3 in. wide and 1½ in. thick. This base is fastened to the trestles and divided into four sections, the sections on each side of the center being 4 ft. long.

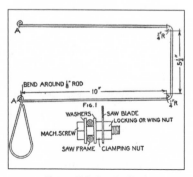

Frame Made of a Rod

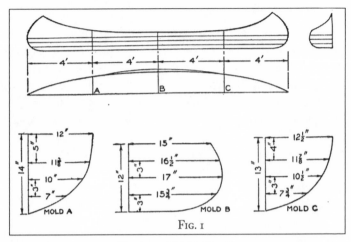

Canoe and Molds Details

The next thing to be considered are the molds (Fig. 3). These are made of 1-in. material. Scrap pieces may be found that can be used for these molds. The dimensions given in Fig. 1 are for one-half of each form as shown in Fig. 3, under their respective letters. The molds are then temporarily attached to the base on the division lines.

Proceed to make the curved ends as shown in Fig. 4. Two pieces of straight-grained green elm, 32 in. long, 1¾ in. wide and 1 in. thick, will be required. The elm can be obtained from a carriage or blacksmith's shop.

The pieces are bent by wrapping a piece of wire around the upper end and baseboard. The joint between the curved piece and the base is temporary. Place a stick between the wires and twist them until the required shape is secured. If the wood does not bend readily, soak it in boiling water. The vertical height and the horizontal length of this bend are shown in Fig. 4. The twisted wire will give the right curve and hold the wood in shape until it is dry.

The gunwales are the long pieces B, Fig. 2, at the top of the canoe. These are made of strips of ash, 15 ft. long, 1 in.

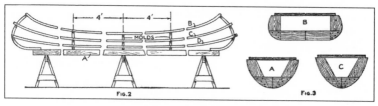

Shaping the Canoe

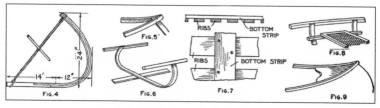

Construction of the Various Parts

wide and 1 in. thick. Fasten them temporarily to the molds, taking care to have them snugly fit the notches shown. The ends fit over the outside of the stem and stern pieces and are cut to form a sharp point, as shown in Fig. 5. The ends of the gunwales are fastened permanently to the upper ends of the bent stem and stern pieces with several screws.

Two other light strips, C and D, Fig. 2, are temporarily put in, and evenly spaced between the gunwales and the bottom board. These strips are used to give the form to the ribs, and are removed when they have served their purpose.

The ribs are now put in place. They are formed of strips of well seasoned elm or hickory, soaked in boiling water until they bend without breaking or cracking. Each rib should be 1½ in. wide, ⅜ in. thick and long enough to reach the distance between the gunwales after the bend is made. The ribs are placed 1 in. apart. Begin by placing a rib in the center of the base and on the upper side. Nail it temporarily, yet securely, and then curve the ends and place them inside of the gunwales, as shown in Fig. 6. Fasten the ends of the rib to the gunwales with 1-in. galvanized brads. This method is used in placing all the ribs. When the ribs are set, remove the pieces C and D, Fig. 2, and the molds.

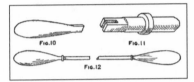

Paddle Parts

A strip is now put in to take the place of the base. This strip is 1¾ in. wide, ½ in. thick and long enough to reach the entire length of the bottom of the canoe. It is fastened with screws on the inside, as shown in Fig. 7, and the ends are lap-jointed to the stem and stern pieces as shown in Fig. 4. When this piece is fastened in place, the base can be removed. The seats are attached as shown in Fig. 8, and the small pieces for each end are fitted as shown in Fig. 9.

The frame of the canoe is now ready to be covered. This will require 5½ yd. of extra-heavy canvas. Turn the framework of the canoe upside down and place the canvas on it. The center of the canvas is located and tacked to the center strip of the canoe at the points where ribs are attached. Copper tacks should be used. The canvas is then tacked to the ribs, beginning at the center rib and working toward each end, carefully drawing the canvas as tightly as possible and keeping it straight. At the ends the canvas is split in the center and lapped over the bent wood. The surplus canvas is cut off. A thin coat of glue is put on, to shrink the cloth and make it water-proof.

The glue should be powdered and brought into liquid form in a double boiler. A thin coat of this is applied with a paintbrush. A small keel made of a strip of wood is placed on the bottom to protect it when making a landing on sand and stones in shallow water. When the glue is thoroughly dry the canvas is covered with two coats of paint, made up in any color with the best lead and boiled linseed oil. The inside is coated with spar varnish to give it a wood color.

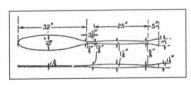

A Single Paddle

The paddles may be made up in two ways, single or double. The double paddle has a hickory pole, 7 ft. long and 2 in. in diameter, for its center part. The paddle is made as shown in Fig. 10, of ash or cypress. It is 12 in. long, and 8 in. wide at the widest part. The paddle end fits into a notch cut in the end of the pole (Fig. 11). A shield is made of a piece of tin or rubber and placed around the pole near the paddle to prevent the water from running to the center as the pole is tipped from side to side. The complete paddle is shown in Fig. 12. A single paddle is made as shown in Fig. 13. This is made of ash or any other tough wood. The dimensions given in the sketch are sufficient without a description.

How to Make a Cannon

A cannon like the one in the cut may be made from a piece of 1-in. hydraulic pipe, A, with a steel sleeve, B, and a long thread plug, C. Be sure to get hydraulic pipe, or double extra heavy, as it is sometimes called, as common gas pipe is entirely too light for this purpose. Don't

have the pipe too long or the cannon will not make as much noise. Seven or eight inches is about the right length for a 1-in. bore. Screw the plug and pipe up tightly and then drill a 1⁄16-in. fuse hole at D.

If desired the cannon may be mounted on a block of wood, F, by means of a U-bolt or large staple, E.—Contributed by Carson Birkhead, Moorhead, Miss.

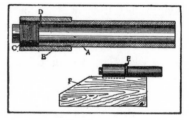

Toy Cannon

How to Make a Finger Ring

While the wearing of copper rings for rheumatism may be a foolish notion, yet there is a certain galvanic action set up by the

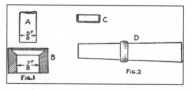

Tools for Forming the Ring

contact of the acid in the system of the afflicted person with the metal of the ring. Apart from this, however, a ring may be made from any metal, such as copper, brass and silver, if such metals are in plate or sheet form, by the following method:

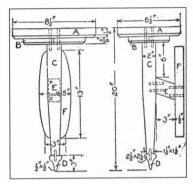

Details of the Wall Bracket

All the tools necessary are a die and punch which are simple to make and will form a ring that will fit the average finger. Take a ¾-in. nut, B, Fig. 1, and drill out the threads. This will leave a clear hole, ⅞ in. in diameter, or a hole drilled the desired size in a piece of iron plate will do as well. Countersink the top of the hole so that the full diameter of the countersink will be 1¼ in. This completes the die. The punch A, is made of a piece of ⅝-in. round iron, slightly rounded on the end so that it will not cut through the metal disk. The dimensions shown in Fig. 1 can be changed to suit the size of the finger to be fitted.

The metal used should be about ¹⁄₁₆ in. thick and 1¼ in. in diameter. Anneal it properly by heating and plunging in water. Lay it on the die so that it will fit nicely in the countersink and drive it through the hole by striking the punch with a hammer. Hold the punch as nearly central as possible when starting to drive the metal through the hole. The disk will come out pan shaped, C, and it is only necessary to remove the bottom of the pan to have a band which will leave a hole ⅝ in. in diameter and 1¼ in. wide. Place the band, D, Fig. 2, on a stick so that the edges can be filed and rounded to shape. Finish with fine emery cloth and polish. Brass rings can be plated when finished.—Contributed by H. W. Hankin, Troy, N. Y.

HOW TO MAKE A HECTOGRAPH

A hectograph is very simply and easily made and by means of it many copies of writing

Making Copies with the Hectograph

can be obtained from a single original.

Make a tray of either tin or paste-board, a little larger than the sheet of paper you ordinarily use and about ½ in. deep. Soak 1 oz. of gelatine in cold water over night and in the morning pour off the water. Heat 6½ oz. of glycerine to about 200 deg. F. on a water bath, and add the gelatine. This should give a clear glycerine solution of gelatine.

Place the tray so that it is perfectly level and pour in the gelatinous composition until it is nearly level with the edge of the tray. Cover it so the cover does not touch the surface of the composition and let it stand six hours, when it will be ready for use.

Make the copy to be reproduced on ordinary paper with aniline ink; using a steel pen, and making the lines rather heavy so they have a greenish color in the light. A good ink may be made of methyl violet 2 parts, alcohol 2 parts, sugar 1 part, glycerine 4 parts, and water 24 parts. Dissolve the violet in the alcohol mixed with the glycerine; dissolve the sugar in the water and mix both solutions.

When the original copy of the writing is ready moisten the surface of the hectograph slightly with a sponge, lay the copy face down upon it and smooth down, being careful to exclude all air bubbles and not shifting the paper. Leave it nearly a minute and raise one corner and strip it from the pad, where will remain a reversed copy of the inscription.

Immediately lay a piece of writing paper of the right size on the pad, smooth it down and then remove as before. It will bear a perfect copy of the original. Repeat the operation until the number of copies desired is obtained or until the ink on the pad is exhausted. Fifty or more copies can be obtained from a single original.

When through using the hectograph wash it off with a moist sponge, and it will be ready for future use. If the surface is impaired at any time it can be remelted in a water bath and poured into a tray as before, if it has not absorbed too much ink.

How to Make a Hygrometer

Mount a wire on a board which is used for a base and should be ⅜ by 4 by 8 in., as shown in the sketch. A piece of catgut—a string used on a violin will do—is suspended from the bent end of the wire. A hand or pointer is cut from a piece of tin and secured to the catgut string about ½ in. from the base. A small piece of wood and some glue will

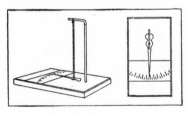

Simple Hygrometer

fasten the pointer to the string. The scale is marked on a piece of cardboard, which is fastened to the base and protected with a piece of glass.—Contributed by J. Thos. Rhamstine.

How to Make a Minnow Trap

Glass minnow traps that will give as good service as those purchased at the tackle store can made without difficulty. If a trap should be banged carelessly against the side of the boat or some other obstruction and smashed, instead of spending several dollars to replace it, a half hour's time will turn out a new one just as good, says a correspondent of Outing.

A trap of this kind can be made from an ordinary fruit jar such as used in putting up preserves, either of one or two-quart capacity. A one-quart jar gives good results, but if the bait to be caught is of fairly large size, the two-quart size may be used. As the jars have the same style top they can be used interchangeably with one mouthpiece.

The mouthpiece is made of a round-neck bottle of which

the glass is colorless and rather thin. If the neck of the bottle is cut at the right point, it makes a glass funnel that will just fit into the fruit jar. The funnel forms the mouth of the trap. Put the neck of the bottle into the fruit jar and mark the glass with a file where the bottle and jar meet. Make as deep a cut as possible with a file around the bottle on the mark and place two turns of a yarn string saturated in kerosene around just below the cut when the bottle is standing in an upright position. Set fire to the string and turn the bottle from side to side to distribute the heat evenly, then when the string has burned out, plunge the bottle in cold water and it will separate on the cut.

Bind some copper wire around the neck of the jar so that three ends will project ½ in. or more. These are bent down over the funnel when put into the jar, forming clamps to hold it in place. The copper wire can be bent many times in emptying or baiting the trap without breaking.

Two copper wire bands are tied tightly around the jar about 3 in. apart. They should be twisted tight with a pair of pliers and the ends joined, forming a ring for attaching a cord.

For catching "Kellies" or "killies," bait the trap with crushed clams or salt-water mussels and for fresh water shines use mincemeat or bread crumbs and do not spill any bait outside of the trap. Leave the trap down ten to fifteen minutes and when resetting it after emptying, put back one or two of the victims, as the others enter more readily if they see some of their companions ahead of them.

How to Make a Portfolio

Secure a piece of Russian modeling calf leather of a size equal to 12 by 16 in. Make a paper pattern of the size indicated in the accompanying drawing, putting in the design.

The necessary tools consist of a stick with a straight edge and a tool with an end shaped like that of a nutpick. A nutpick with a V-shaped point will do if the sharpness is smoothed off by means of a piece of emery paper, so that it will indent without cutting the leather. These tools can be bought for this special purpose, but are not essential for this piece if the nutpick is at hand. There will also be needed a level, non-absorbent surface upon which to lay the leather while working it. A piece of thick glass, metal, or marble will serve.

Begin work by moistening the leather on the back side with a sponge or cloth. Moisten as much as you dare and still not have the moisture show on the face side. Next place the leather on the glass, face up,

and, holding the pattern firmly in place so that it will not slip— if possible get some one to hold the pattern for you—place the straight edge on the straight lines and mark out or indent. After this has been done, mark over the design. A pencil may be used the first time over.

The pattern is now to be removed and all the lines gone over with the tool to make them deep and uniform.

The surplus stock around the edges may not be cut off. A neat way to finish the edges is to punch a series of holes entirely around through

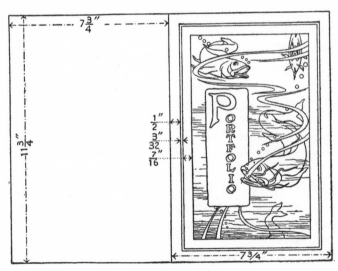

Portfolio Design

which a thin leather thong may be laced. If it is desired to "line" the inside, this should be done before the holes are punched or the lacing done.

HOW TO MAKE AN ELECTRIC TOASTER

The electric toaster shown in the sketch is not hard to make. The framework comprising the base and the two uprights may be made either of hardwood or asbestos board, says Popular Electricity. If constructed of the former, the portion of the base under the coil, and the inside surfaces of the two uprights should be covered with a ⅛-in. sheet of well made asbestos paper, or thin asbestos board may be substituted for this lining. Asbestos board is to be preferred, and this material in almost any degree of hardness may be purchased. It can be worked into shape and will hold wood-screws. The detail drawing gives all dimensions necessary to shape the wood or asbestos board.

After preparing the base and uprights, drill 15 holes, ¼ in. deep, into the inside face of each upright to support the No. 6 gauge wires shown. The wires at the top and bottom for holding the resistance wire are covered with asbestos paper and the holes for these wires are ¾ in. from the top and bottom, respectively, of the uprights. The wires that form the cage about the heater coil and are used for a support for the toast are 15 pieces of No. 6 gauge iron wire each 8 in. long. The screws that hold the uprights in position should have the heads countersunk on the under side of the base. The binding-posts should now be set in position and their protecting covering containing the reinforced cord left until the other parts are finished.

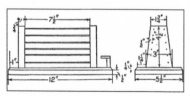

Detail of Toaster

To assemble, secure one upright in position using 1½-in. wood-screws. Place the other upright where it belongs without fastening it and put the stretcher wires for holding the resistance wire in place. Put the asbestos paper on these and with the assistance of a helper begin winding on the heater coil. Use 80 ft. of 18-percent No. 22 gauge German-silver wire. Wind the successive turns of wire so they will not touch each other and fasten at each end with a turn or two of No. 16 gauge copper wire. When this is complete have the helper hold the stretcher wires while you tip the unfastened upright out and insert the wires of the cage, then fasten the upright in place.

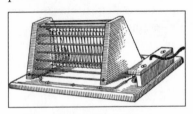

Toaster Complete

The wire from the binding-posts to the coil may be what is known as underwriters' wire or asbestos-covered wire No. 14 gauge, which is held in place by double-headed tacks containing an insulation at the head. These may be procured from electrical supply houses.

Connect the reinforced cord and terminals to the binding screws and fasten the cover in place. This toaster will take four amperes on 110-volt circuit.

SMALL ELECTRICAL HYDROGEN GENERATOR

A small hydrogen generator may be made from a fruit jar, A (see sketch), with two tubes, B and C, soldered in the top. The plates E can be made of tin or galvanized iron, and should be separated about ⅛ in by small pieces of wood. One of these plates is connected to metal top, and the wire from the other passes through the tube B, which is filled with melted rosin or wax, to make it airtight. This wire connects to one side of a battery of two cells, the other wire being soldered to the metal top of the jar, as shown. The jar is partly filled with a very dilute solution of sulphuric acid, about 1 part of acid to 20 of water.

When the current of electricity passes between the plates E, hydrogen gas is generated, which rises and passes through the rubber hose D, into the receiver G. This is a wide-mouth bottle, which is filled with water and inverted over a pan of water, F. The gas bubbling up displaces the water and fills the bottle.

If the receiver is removed when half full of gas, the remaining space will be filled with air, which will mix with the gas and form an explosive mixture. If a lighted match is then held near the mouth of the bottle a sharp report will be heard.

If the bottle is fitted with a cork containing two wires nearly touching, and the apparatus connected with an induction coil, in such a manner that a spark will be produced inside the bottle, the explosion will blow out the cork or possibly break the bottle. Caution should be used to avoid being struck by pieces of flying glass if this experiment is tried, and

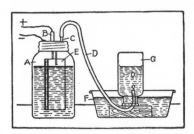

Hydrogen Generator

under no condition should a lighted match or spark be brought near the end of the rubber hose D, as the presence of a little air in the generator will make an explosive mixture which would probably break the jar.

To Make a Magazine Binder

Get ½ yd. of cloth, one shoestring, a pasteboard box for covers, and some heavy paper. Cut the pasteboard into two covers, ¼ in. larger all around than the magazine, except at the back with which they should be even. Next cut a strip 1 in. wide off the back of each cover. Place the covers on the cloth, Fig. 1, with the back edges ¼ in. farther apart than the thickness of the volume to be bound. Cut the cloth around the covers, leaving 1½ in. margin. Paste the cloth on the covers, as they lay, and turn over the 1½ in. margin, pasting down smoothly. Cut a piece of stiff paper to fit and paste on the back. Take a piece of cloth as wide as the cover, and long enough to extend over the back

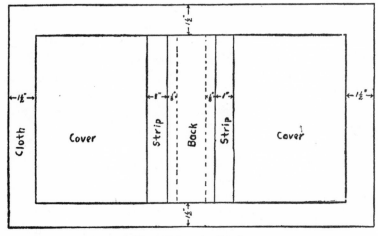

Plan of Magazine Binder

and 1½ in. beyond each "strip." Paste on to hold all together. Two pieces of paper the exact size of the magazine, pasted on the inside of each cover protects the cloth, and adds to the appearance. Let dry slowly.

With backs and edges of magazines even, place in a vise and set up tight allowing ¾ in. from back to show above the vise. Bore three $\frac{3}{16}$-in. holes ½ in. from the back, one in the middle, the other two 1½ in. from each end. Make corresponding holes in the strips of the binder and use the shoestring to complete as in Fig. 2.

A piece of wire solder makes a good temporary spline for the draftsman.

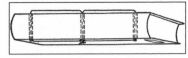

Magazine Binder Complete

ANIMAL TRAPS

A GOOD MOUSE TRAP

When opening a tomato or other small can, cut the cover crossways from side to side making four triangular pieces in the top. Bend the four ends outward and remove the contents, wash clean and dry and then bend the four ends inward, leaving a hole about ¾ in. in diameter in the center. Drop in a piece of bread and lay the can down upon its side and the trap is ready for use. The mouse can get in but he cannot get out.— Contributed by E. J. Crocker, Victor, Colo.

A HOME-MADE RABBIT TRAP

A good serviceable rabbit trap can be made by sinking a common dry goods box in the ground to within 6 in. of its top. A hole 6 or 7 in. square is cut in each end level with the earth's surface and boxes 18 in. long that will just fit are set in, hung on pivots, with the longest end outside, so they will lie horizontal. A rabbit may now look through the two tubes, says the American Thresherman. The bait is hung on a string from the top of the large box so that it may be seen and smelled from the outside. The rabbit naturally goes into the holes and in this trap there is nothing to awaken his suspicion. He smells the bait, squeezes along past the center

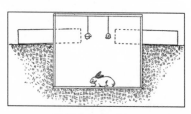

Rabbit in the Trap

of the tube, when it tilts down and the game is shot into the pit, the tube righting itself at once for another catch. The top and sides of the large box may be covered with leaves, snow or anything to hide it. A door placed in the top will enable the trapper to take out the animals. By placing a little hay or other food in the bottom of the box the trap need not be visited oftener than once a week.

A Novel Rat Trap

A boy, while playing in the yard close to a grain house, dug a hole and buried an old-fashioned fruit jug or jar that  his mother had thrown away, says the Iowa Homestead. The top part of the jug was left uncovered as shown in the sketch, and a hole was broken in it just above the ground. The boy then placed some shelled corn in the bottom, put a board on top, and weighted it with a heavy stone.

The jug had been forgotten for several days when a farmer found it, and, wondering what it was, he raised the board and found nine full-grown rats and four, mice in the bottom. The trap has been in use for some time and is opened every day or two and never fails to have from one to six rats or mice in it.

Home-Made Dog Cart

The accompanying photograph shows a boy with his "dogmobile." The photograph was taken when they were on a new pavement which had 2 in. of sand left by the pavers and a grade of 6 percent. The machine is nothing more than a boy's rubber-tired wagon on which are mounted a box for a seat and a wheel steering device extending above and below the board of the wagon. The front

Dog-Power Cart

wheels are guided by ropes attached from each end of the axle and a few turns around the lower end of the steering rod. A pair of shafts are attached to the rear, into which the dog is harnessed.

HOMEMADE MOUSETRAP

Bore a 1-in. hole, about 2 in. deep, in a block of wood and drive a small nail with a sharp point at an angle so it will project into the hole about half way between the top and bottom, and in the center of the hole, as shown. File the end very sharp and bend it down

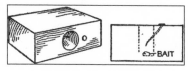

Hole in Wood Block

so that when the mouse pushes its head past it in trying to get the bait at the bottom of the hole, the sharp point will catch it when it tries to back out. Almost anyone can make this trap in a short time, and it will catch the mice as surely as a more elaborate trap.

HOW TO MAKE A SELF-SETTING RABBIT TRAP

Secure a good-sized box, say, 1 ft. high, 1½ ft. wide, and 3ft. long; and to the bottom, about 10 in. from one end, fasten a 2-in. square piece, A, Fig. 1, extending the width of the box. Place a 10-in. board sloping

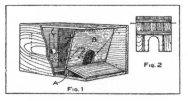

Self-Setting Trap

from the end of the box to the cleat A. The swing door B, Fig. 1, is made as shown in Fig. 2, which represents the back side of the door. Sheet metal or tin is cut to the proper size and tacked around the edge of the hole. This prevents the animal from gnawing its way out, also provides a way to make the hole of different sizes for squirrels or other animals. The hole in the door should be about 2 in. wide and 4 in. high for rabbits. The door is made to swing freely on two large nails driven through the sides of the box. The hole in the door being only large enough to admit a small portion of the rabbit's head, the rabbit will push its way through to the bait, causing the door to swing back and up, and it will close by its own weight when the animal is inside. A small door is provided in the other end to remove the animals caught.

The advantage of this trap is that where one animal is caught others are liable to follow, and several rabbits will be trapped at a time. Then, too, the rabbits are not harmed in any way as they would be if caught in an ordinary trap.—Contributed by H. F. Church, Alexandria, Va.

How to Make a Trap for Rabbits, Rats and Mice

From an old 6-in. pine fence board cut off four pieces 2½ ft. long and one 6 in. square for the end of the trap and another 4 in. by 8 in. for the door. Use old boards, as new boards scare rabbits.

Figure 1 shows how the box is made. It should be 4 in. wide and 6 in. high on the inside. The top and bottom boards project 1 in. beyond the side boards at the back and the end board is set in. The top board should be 2 in. shorter than the sides at the front. Nail a strip on the top board back of the door and one on the bottom board so the game connot push the door open from inside the trap and get out.

In the middle of the top board bore a hole and put a crotched stick in for the lever to rest on. Bore another hole in the top of the door for the lever to pass through. Two inches from

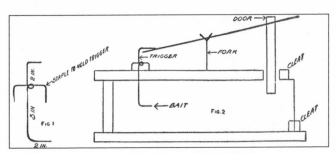

A Good Trap for small Animals

the back of the box bore a hole for the trigger, which should be made out of heavy wire in the manner shown in Fig. 2. The door of the trap must work easily and loosely.

How to Rid Your Yard of Cats

The following is a description of a device I built at my home in Brooklyn, which not only gave us relief from the nightly feline concerts, but also furnished much amusement to my friends.

I first ran two bare copper wires along the top of the fence about 1 in. apart, fastening them down with small staples, care being taken that they did not touch. To the ends of these wires I fastened ordinary insulated bell wire, running them to the house and connecting them to the upper binding-post of an induction coil; I then ran a wire from the lower binding-post of my coil through the batteries back to the other lower binding-post of coil, breaking the circuit by putting in an ordinary switch. The more batteries used, the stronger the current. The switch should always be left open, as it uses up the current very rapidly.

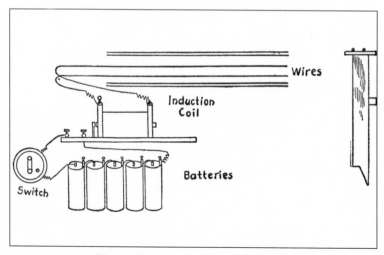

Electric Apparatus for Driving Away Cats

When "tabby" is well on the wires I close the switch and she goes the length of the fence in bounds, often coming back to see what the trouble is, thus receiving another shock.—Contributed by Charles L. Pultz.

A gouge may be used as a substitute bit if a proper sized bit is not at hand. The gouge can be placed in the brace the same as a bit.

Novel Mousetrap

A piece of an old bicycle tire and a glass fruit jar are the only materials required for making this trap. Push one end of the tire into the hole, making sure that there is a space left at the end so that the mice can get in.

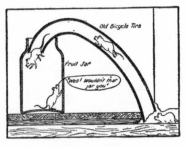

Old Bicycle Tire

Fruit Jar

"Well! Wouldn't that jar you"

A Baitless Trap

Then bend the other end down into a fruit jar or other glass jar. Bait may be placed in the jar if desired, although this is not necessary.—Contributed by Geo. O. McVicker, North Bend, Neb.

CA brilliant polish may be given to tarnished nickel by immersing in alcohol and 2 per cent of sulphuric acid from 5 to 15 seconds. Take out, wash in running water, rinse in alcohol, and rub dry with linen cloth.

Trap for Small Animals

 This is a box trap with glass sides and back, the panes of glass being held in place by brads placed on both sides. The animal does not fear to enter the box, because he can see through it; when he enters, however, and touches the bait the lid is released and, dropping, shuts him in. This is one of the easiest traps to build and is usually successful.

MAGIC

AN OPTICAL ILLUSION

When looking at the accompanying sketch you will say that the letters are alternately inclined to the right and left. They are not so and can be proved by measuring the distance of the top and bottom of any vertical strokes from the edge of the entire block. They will be found to be exactly the same distance. Or take any of the horizontal strokes of the four letters and see how far their extremities are from the top and bottom of the entire block. It will be found that a line joining the extremities of the strokes are strictly parallel to the top or bottom and that they are not on a slant at all. It is the slant of the numerous short lines that go to make up the letter as a whole that deceives the eye.

AN OPTICAL TOP

One of the latest optical delusions, and one not easy to explain, is Benham's color top. Cut out the black and white

An Optical Top

The Cord Is Not a Spiral

disk shown in the figure, and paste on a piece of stiff cardboard. Trim the edges of the cardboard to match the shape of the disk, and make a pinhole in the center. Cut the pin in half and push it through from the under side until the head of the pin touches the cardboard. Spin slowly in a strong light and some of the lines will appear colored. The colors appear different to different people, and are changed by reversing the rotation.

ANOTHER OPTICAL ILLUSION

After taking a look at the accompanying illustration you will be positive that the cords shown run in a spiral toward the center, yet it shown a series of perfect circles of cords placed one inside the other. You can test this yourself in a moment with a pair of compasses, or, still more simply, by laying a point of a pencil on any part of the cord and following it round. Instead of approaching or receding from the center in a continuous line, as in the case of a spiral, you will find the pencil returning to the point from which it started.

OPTICAL ILLUSIONS

By giving the page a revolving or rinsing motion the three circular figures printed on the next page appear to rotate. The best effect will be produced by

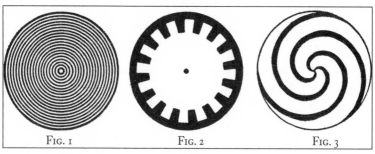

FIG. 1 FIG. 2 FIG. 3

Move These Figures Rapidly with a Rinsing Motion

laying the book down flat on the desk or table and revolving, first in one direction and then in the opposite direction, in such a way that any given point on the page will describe a circle of about ½ in. diameter. Fig. 1 then appears to rotate in the same direction as the revolution; Fig. 2 appears to revolve in the opposite direction, and Fig. 3 appears to revolve sometimes in the same direction and at other times in the opposite direction.

A curious effect can be produced with Fig. 1 by covering up Figs. 2 and 3 with a piece of plain paper and laying a coin or other small object on the paper. If the vision is then concentrated on the coin or other object while same is being revolved, Fig. 1 will be seen to rotate.

OPTICAL ILLUSIONS

The accompanying sketch shows two optical illusions, the first having a perfect circle on the outside edge appears to be flattened at the points A, and the arcs of the circle, B, appear to be more rounding. In the second figure the circle appears to have an oval from with the distance from C to C greater than from D to D. A compass applied to the circles in either figures will show that they are perfectly round.—Contributed

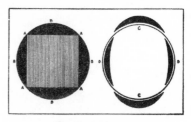

The Two Illusions

by Norman S. Brown, Chippewa Falls, Wis.

CARD TRICK WITH A TAPERED DECK

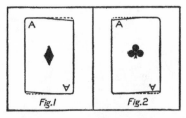

Cards from a Tapered Deck

Another simple trick to perform but one not easily detected, is executed by using a tapered deck of cards as shown in Fig. 1. A cheap deck of cards is evened up square, fastened in a vise and planed along the edge in such a manner that all the pack will be tapered about ¹⁄₁₆ in. This taper is exaggerated in the illustration which shows one card that has been turned end for end.

It is evident that any card reversed in this way can be easily separated from the other cards in the pack, which makes it possible to perform the following trick: The performer spreads the cards out, fan-like, and asks an observer to withdraw a card, which is then replaced in any part of the pack. After thoroughly shuffling the cards the performer then holds the deck in both hands behind his back and pronouncing a few magic words, produces the card selected in one hand and the rest of the pack in the other. This is accomplished by simply turning the deck end for end while the observer is looking at his card, thus bringing the wide end of the selected card at the narrow end of the pack when it is replaced. The hands are placed behind the back for a double purpose, as the feat then seems more marvelous and the observers are not allowed to see how it is done.

In prize games, players having the same score are frequently called upon to cut for low to determine which shall be the winner, but a fairer way is to cut for high as a person familiar with the trick shown in Fig. 2 can cut the cards at the ace, deuce, or three spot, nearly every time, especially if the deck is a new one. This is done by simply pressing on the top of the deck as shown, before cutting, thus causing the increased ink surface of the high cards to adhere to the adjacent ones. A little practice will soon enable one to cut low nearly every time, but the cards must be grasped lightly and the experiment should be performed with a new deck to obtain successful results.—Contributed by D. B. J., Chicago.

COIN AND TUMBLER TRICK

The accompanying sketch shows how a good trick may be easily performed by any one. Lay a piece of heavy paper that is free from creases on a board or table. Secure three tumblers that are alike and stick a piece of the same heavy paper over the openings in two of them, neatly trimming it all around the edges so as to leave nothing of the paper for any one to see. Make three covers of paper as shown in Fig. 1 to put over the tumblers. Place three coins on the sheet of paper, then the tumblers with covers on top of the coins the unprepared tumbler being in the middle. Now lift the covers off the end tumblers, and you will see that the paper on the openings covers the coins. Replace the covers, lift the middle one, and a coin will be seen under the tumbler, as the opening of this tumbler is not covered. Drop the cover back again and lift the other tumblers and covers bodily, so that the spectators can see the coins, remarking at the same time that you can make them vanish from one to the other. The openings of the tumblers must never be exposed so that any one can see them, and a safe way to do this is to keep them level with the table.

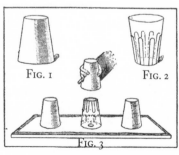

This is a Good Trick

DISAPPEARING COIN

While this is purely a sleight-of-hand trick, it will take very little practice to cause the coin to disappear instantly. Take a quarter of a dollar between the thumb and finger, as shown, and by a rapid twist of the fingers whirl the coin and at the same time close the hand,

and the coin will disappear up your coat sleeve. On opening the hand the coin will not be seen. Take three quarters and hold one in the palm of the left hand, place the other two, one between the thumb and finger of each hand, then give the coin in the right hand a whirl, as described, closing both hands quickly. The coin in the right hand will disappear up your sleeve, and the left hand on being unclosed will contain two quarters, while the one in the right shall have disappeared.

MAGIC SPIRIT HAND

The magic hand made of wax is given to the audience for examination, also a board which is suspended by four pieces of common picture-frame wire. The hand is placed upon the board and answers, by rapping, any question asked by members of the audience. The hand and the board may be examined at any time and yet the rapping can be continued, though surrounded by the audience.

The Magic Wand, London, gives the secret of this spirit hand as follows: The hand is prepared by concealing in the wrist a few soft iron plates, the wrist being afterwards bound with black velvet as shown in Fig. 1. The board is hollow, the top being made of thin veneer (Fig. 2). A small magnet, A, is connected to a small flat pocket lamp battery, B. The board is suspended by four lengths of picture-frame wire one of which, E, is connected to the

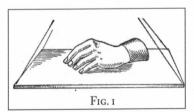

FIG. 1

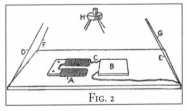

FIG. 2

Wax Hand on Board and Electrical Connections

battery and another, D, to the magnet. The other wires, F and G, are only holding wires. All the wires are fastened to a small ornamental switch, H, which is fitted with a connecting plug at the top. The plug can be taken out or put in as desired.

The top of the board must be made to open or slide off so that when the battery is exhausted a new one can be installed. Everything must be firmly fixed to the board and the hollow space filled in with wax, which will make the board sound solid when tapped.

In presenting the trick, the performer gives the hand and board with wires and switch for examination, keeping the plug concealed in his right hand. When receiving the board back, the plug is secretly pushed into the switch, which is held in the right hand. The hand is then placed on the board over the magnet. When the performer wishes the hand to move he pushes the plug in, which turns on the current and causes the magnet to attract the iron in the wrist, and will, therefore, make the hand rap.

The switch can be made similar to an ordinary push button so the rapping may be easily controlled without detection by the audience.

MOVING A COIN UNDER A GLASS

Place a penny or a dime on a table cloth, towel or napkin and cover it over with a glass in such a way that the glass will rest upon two 25 or 50-cent pieces as shown in the sketch. The coin is made to come forth without touching it or sliding a stick under the edge of the glass. It is only necessary to claw the cloth near the glass with the nail of the forefinger.

The cloth will produce a movement that will slide the coin to the edge and from under the glass.

Removing the Coin

OLD-TIME MAGIC

Balancing Forks on a Pin Head

Two, three and four common table forks can be made to balance on a pin head as follows: Procure an empty bottle

and insert a cork in the neck. Stick a pin in the center of this cork so that the end will be about 1½ in. above the top. Procure another cork about 1 in. in diameter by 1¾ in. long. The forks are now stuck into the latter cork at equal distances apart, each having the same angle from the cork. A long needle with a good sharp point is run through the cork with the forks and ½ in. of the needle end allowed to project through the lower end.

The point of the needle now may be placed on the pin head. The forks will balance and if given a slight push they will appear to dance. Different angles of the forks will produce various feats of balancing.—Contributed by O. E. Tronnes, Wilmette, Ill.

Trick with a Coin in a Wine Glass

The accompanying sketch shows a trick of removing a dime from the bottom of an old fashioned wine glass without touching the coin. The dime is first placed in the bottom of the glass and then a silver quarter dropped in on top. The quarter will not go all the way down. Blow hard into the glass

in the position shown and the dime will fly out and strike the blower on the nose.

Untying-a-Knot Trick

Tie a double knot in a silk handkerchief, as shown in the accompanying sketch and tighten the last tie a little by slightly drawing the two upper ends; then continue to tighten much more, pulling vigorously at the first corner of the hand-kerchief, and as this end belongs

to the same corner it cannot be pulled much without loosening the twisted line of the knot to become a straight line. The other corner forms a slip knot on the end, which can be drawn out without disturbing the form, or apparent security of the knot, at the moment when you cover the knot with the unused part of the handkerchief.

When the trick is to be performed, tie two or three very hard knots that are tightly drawn and show your audience that they are not easy to untie. The slip knot as described then must be made in apparently the same way and untied with the thumb while the knot is in the folds of the handkerchief.

The Disappearing Coin

This is an uncommon trick, entirely home-made and yet the results are as startling as in many of the professional tricks. A small baking-powder can is employed to vanish the coin, which should be marked by one of the audience for identification. Cut a slot in the bottom on the side of the can, as shown in Fig. 1. This slot should be just large enough for the coin that is used to pass through freely, and to have its lower edge on a level with the bottom of the can.

The nest or series of boxes in which the coin is afterwards found should consist of four small sized flat pasteboard boxes square or rectangular shaped and furnished with hinged covers. The smallest need be no larger than necessary to hold the coin and each succeeding box should be just large enough to hold the next smaller one which in turn contains the others.

A strip of tin about 1 by 1¾ in. is bent in the shape as shown in Fig. 2 to serve as a guide for the coin through the various boxes. This guide is inserted about ⅛ in. in the smallest box between the cover and the box and three rubber bands wrapped around the box as indicated. This box is then enclosed in the next larger

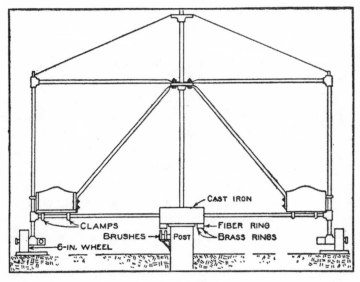

Details of the Swing

box, the guide being allowed to project between the box and the cover, and the necessary tension is secured by three rubber bands around the box as before. In like manner the remaining boxes are adjusted so that finally the prepared nest of boxes appears as in Fig. 3.

The coin can easily be passed into the inner box through the tin guide, then the guide can be withdrawn which permits the respective boxes to close and the rubber bands hold each one in a closed position.

The performer comes forward with the tin can in his right hand, the bottom of the can in his palm with the slot at the right side. He removes the cover with the left hand and passes his wand around the inner part of the can which is then turned upside down to prove that it contains nothing.

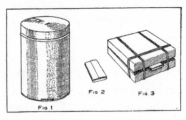

Appliances for the Disappearing Coin

The marked coin is dropped into the can by some one in the audience. The cover is replaced and the can shaken so the coin will rattle within. The shaking of the can is continued until the coin has slipped through the slot into his palm. The can is then placed on the table with his left hand. Then apparently he looks for something to cover the can. This is found to be a handkerchief which was previously prepared on another table concealing the nest of boxes. The coin in the right hand is quickly slipped into the guide of the nest of boxes, which was placed in an upright position, and the guide withdrawn, and dropped on the table. The performer, while doing this, is explaining that he is looking for a suitable cover for the can, but as he cannot find one he takes the handkerchief instead. The handkerchief is spread over the can and then he brings the nest of boxes. He explains how he will transfer the coin and passes his wand from the can to the boxes. The can is then shown to be empty and the boxes given to one in the audience to be opened.

They will be greatly surprised to find the marked coin within the innermost box.

A Handkerchief Mended after Being Cut and Torn

Two persons are requested to come forward from the audience to hold the four corners of a handkerchief. Then beg several other handkerchiefs from the audience and place them on the one held by the two persons. When several handkerchiefs have been accumulated, have some one person draw out one from the bunch and examine for any marks that will determine that this handkerchief is the one to be mended after being mutilated. He, as well as others, are to cut off pieces from this handkerchief and to finally tear it to pieces.

The pieces are then all collected and some magic spirits thrown over the torn and cut parts; tie them in a small package with a ribbon and put them under a glass, which you warm with your hands. After a few seconds' time, you remove the glass, as you have held it all the time, and take the handkerchief and unfold it; everyone will recognize the mark and be amazed not to find a cut or tear in the texture.

This trick is very simple. You have an understanding with some one in the company, who has two handkerchiefs exactly alike and has given one of them to a person behind the curtain; he throws the other, at the time of request for handkerchiefs, on the handkerchiefs held for use in the performance of the trick. You manage to keep this handkerchief where it will be picked out in preference to the others, although pretending to thoroughly mix them up. The person selected to pick out a handkerchief naturally will take the handiest one. Be sure that this is the right one.

When the handkerchief has been torn and folded, put it under the glass, on a table, near a partition or curtain. The table should be made with a hole cut through the top and a small trap door fitted snugly in the hole, so it will appear to be a part of the table top. This trap door is hinged on the under side and opens into the drawer of the table and can be operated by the person behind the curtain who will remove the torn handkerchief and replace it with the good one and then close the trap door by reaching through the drawer of the table.

Changing a Button into a Coin

Place a button in the palm of the left hand, then place a coin between the second and third fingers of the right hand. Keep the right hand faced down and the left hand faced up, so as to conceal the coin and expose the button. With a quick motion bring the left hand under the right, stop quick and the button will go up the right-hand coat sleeve. Press the hands together, allowing the coin to

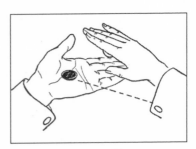

Making the Change

drop into the left hand, then expose again, or rub the hands a little before doing so, saying that you are rubbing a button into a coin.—Contributed by L. E. Parker, Pocatello, Idaho.

THE MAGIC KNOT

This is a very amusing trick which consists of tying one knot with two ends of a handkerchief, and pulling the ends only to untie them again. Take

Typing and Untying a Knot

the two diagonal corners of a handkerchief, one in each hand and throw the main part of the handkerchief over the wrist of the left hand and tie the knot as shown in the illustration. Pull the ends quickly, allowing the loop over the left hand to slip freely, and you will have the handkerchief without any knot.

Cutting a Thread Inside of a Glass Bottle

This is a trick which can only be performed when the sun shines, but it is a good one. Procure a clear glass bottle and stick a pin in the lower end of the cork. Attach a thread to the pin and tie a small weight to

The Glass Directs the Sun's Rays

the end of the thread so it will hang inside the bottle when the cork is in place. Inform your audience that you will sever the thread and cause the weight to drop without removing the cork.

All that is required to perform the feat is to hold a magnifying glass so as to direct the sun's rays on the thread. The thread will quickly burn and the weight fall.

Removing a Key from a Double String

Tie the ends of a 5-ft. string together, making a double line on which a key is placed and the string held as shown by the dotted lines in the sketch. Turn the palms of the hands toward you and reach over with the little finger of the right hand and take hold of the inside line near the left-hand thumb. Reverse the operation and take hold of the inside line near right-hand thumb with the little finger of the left hand. You will then have the string as it appears in the sketch. Quickly let loose of the string with a little finger on one hand and a thumb on the other and pull the string taut. The key will drop from the string.

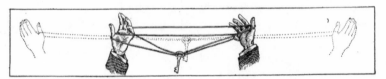

The Key Will Drop from the String

UNIQUE SKILLS

FEAT OF BALANCING ON CHAIRS

Among the numerous physical exercises is the feat of balancing on the two rear legs of a chair while one foot rests on the front park of the seat and the other on the back of the chair. This may appear to be a hard thing to do, yet with a little practice it may be accomplished. This exercise is one of many practiced by the boys of a boys' home for an annual display given by them. A dozen of

the boys will mount chairs at the same time and keep them in balance at the word of a commanding officer.

FINGER MATHEMATICS

BY CHARLES C. BRADLEY

All machinists use mathematics. Ask a machinist what would be the product of 9 times 8 and his ready reply would be 72, but change the figures a little and say 49 times 48 and the chances are that instead of replying at once he will have to figure it out with a pencil. By using the following method it is just as easy to tell at a glance what 99 times 99 are as 9 times 9. You will be able to multiply far beyond your most sanguine expectations.

In the first numbering, begin by holding your hands with

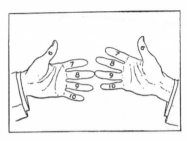

"8 Times 9"

the palms toward the body and make imaginary numbers on the thumbs and fingers as follows: Thumbs, 6; first fingers, 7; second fingers, 8; third fingers, 9, and fourth fingers, 10. Suppose you desire to multiply 8 by 9, put the eighth finger on one hand against the ninth finger of the other hand as shown.

The two joined fingers and all the fingers above them (calling the thumbs fingers) are called the upper fingers and each has a value of ten, which tens are added. All the fingers below the joined fingers are termed the lower fingers, and each of the lower fingers represents a unit value of one. The sum of the units on one hand should be multiplied by the sum of the units on the other hand. The total tens added to this last named sum will give the product desired. Thus: Referring to

above picture or to your hands we find three tens on the left hand and four tens on the right, which would be 70. We also find two units on the left hand and one on the right. Two times one are two, and 70 plus 2 equals 72, or the product of 8 times 9.

Supposing 6 times 6 were the figures. Put your thumbs together; there are no fingers above, so the two thumbs represent two tens or 20; below the thumbs are four units on each hand, which would be 16, and 20 plus 16 equals 36, or the product of 6 times 6.

Supposing 10 times 7 is desired. Put the little finger of the left hand against the first finger of the right hand. At a glance you see seven tens or 70. On the right hand you have three units and on the left nothing. Three times nothing gives you nothing and 70 plus nothing is 70.

In the second numbering, or numbers above 10, renumber your fingers; thumbs, 11; first fingers, 12, etc. Let us multiply 12 by 12.

Put together the tips of the fingers labeled 12. At a glance you see four tens or 40. At this

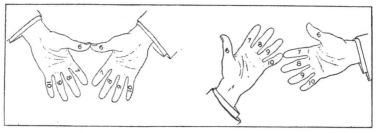

"6 Times 6"   "12 Times 12"

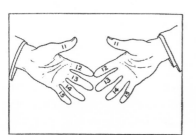

"10 Times 7"

point we leave the method explained in Case 1 and ignore the units (lower fingers) altogether. We go back to the upper fingers again and multiply the number of upper fingers used on the one hand by the number of upper fingers used on the other hand, viz., 2 times 2 equals 4. Adding 4 to 40 gives us 44. We now add 100 (because anything over 10 times 10 would make over 100) and we have 144, the product of 12 times 12.

The addition of 100 is arbitrary, but being simple it saves

time and trouble. Still, if we wish, we might regard the four upper fingers in the above example as four twenties, or 80, and the six lower fingers as six tens, or 60; then returning to the upper fingers and multiplying the two on the right hand by the two on the left we would have 4; hence 80 plus 60 plus 4 equals 144; therefore the rule of adding the lump sum is much the quicker and easier method.

Above 10 times 10 the lump sum to add is 100; above 15 times 15 it is 200; above 20 times 20, 400; 25 times 25, 600, etc., etc., as high as you want to go.

In the third numbering to multiply above 15 renumber your fingers, beginning the thumbs with 16, first finger 17, and so on. Oppose the proper finger tips as before, the upper fingers representing a value of 20. Proceed as in the first numbering and add 200. Take for example 18 times 18.

At a glance we see six twenties plus 2 units on left hand times 2 units on right hand plus 200 equals 324.

In the fourth numbering the fingers are marked, thumbs, 21, first fingers 22, etc., the value of the upper fingers being 20. Proceed as in the second numbering, adding 400 instead of 100.

Above 25 times 25 the upper fingers represent a value of 30 each and after proceeding as in the third numbering you add 600 instead of 200.

This system can be carried as high as you want to go, but you must remember that for figures ending in 1, 2, 3, 4 and 5 proceed as in the second numbering. For figures ending in 6, 7, 8, 9 and 10 the third numbering applies.

Determine the value of the upper fingers whether they represent tens, twenties, thirties, forties, or what. For example, any two figures between 45 and 55, the value of the upper fingers would be 50, which is the half-way point between the two fives. In 82 times 84 the value of the upper fingers would be 80 (the half-way point between the two fives, 75 and 85, being 80). And the lump sum to add.

Just three things to remember: Which numbering is to follow, whether the one described in second or third numbering; the value which the upper fingers have; and, lastly, the lump sum to add, and you will be able to multiply faster and more accurately than you ever dreamed of before.

Fitting a Plug in Different Shaped Holes

A Certain king offered to give the price his liberty if he could whittle a plug that would fit four different-shaped holes, namely: a square hole, a round one, an oblong one and a triangular one, says the Pathfinder. A broomstick was used to make

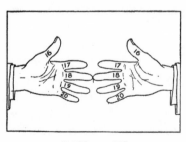

"18 Times 18"

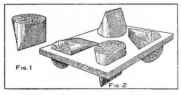

Fits Four Different Shaped Holes

the plug and it was whittled in the shape shown in Fig. 1. The holes in the different places as shown in Fig. 2, were fitted by this one plug.

HOW TO BIND MAGAZINES

An easy way to bind Popular Mechanics in volumes of six months each is to arrange the magazines in order and tie them securely both ways with a strong cord. It is well to put two or three sheets of tough white paper, cut to the size of the pages, at the front and back for fly leaves.

Clamp the whole in a vise or clamp with two strips of wood even with the back edges of the magazines. With a sharp saw cut a slit in the magazines and wood strips about ½ in. deep and slanting as shown at A and B, Fig. 1. Take two strips of stout cloth, about 8 or 10 in. long and as wide as the distance

between the bottoms of the sawed slits. Lay these over the back edge of the pack and tie securely through the slits with a string thread—wrapping and tying several times (C, Fig. 2).

If you have access to a printer's paper knife, trim both ends and the front edge; this makes a much nicer book, but if the paper knife cannot be used, clamp the whole between two boards and saw off the edges, boards and all, smoothly, with a fine saw.

Cut four pieces of cardboard, ¼ in. longer and ¼ in. narrower than the magazines after they have been trimmed. Lay one piece of the board on the book and under the cloth strips. Use ordinary flour paste and paste the strips to the cardboard and then rub paste all over the top of the strips and the board. Rub paste over one side of another piece of board and put it on top of the first board and strips, pressing down firmly so that the strips are held securely between the two boards. Turn the book over and do the same with the other two boards.

After the paste has dried a few minutes take a piece of

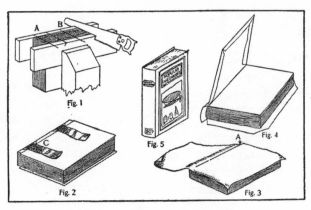

Process of Homemade Binding

strong cloth, duck or linen, fold and cut it 1 in. larger all around than the book, leaving the folded edge uncut. Rub paste over one of the board backs and lay one end of the cloth on it, smoothing and creasing as shown at A, Fig. 3. Turn the book over and paste the other side. The back edges should have a good coat of paste and a strip of paper the width of the thickness of the pack pasted on before pasting the cloth to the second board back.

Cut off the corners and fold over the edges of the cloth, pasting them down (Fig. 4). Rub paste on one side of a fly leaf and press the back down on it. Turn the book over and paste a fly leaf to the other back after the edges of the cloth have been folded down. The backs must not be opened until the fly leaves are thoroughly dry. Trim and tuck in the ends of the strip at the back edge.

When fixed this way your magazines make one of the most valuable volumes you can possibly add to your library of mechanical books.—Contributed by Joseph N. Parker, Bedford City, Va.

HOW TO BORE A SQUARE HOLE

You would not consider it possible to bore a square hole in a piece of cardboard, yet such a thing can be done.

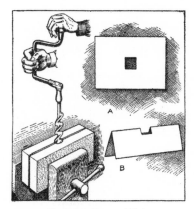

Boring a Square Hole

Take a cardboard or a thin piece of wood, fold and place it between two pieces of board with the fold up; the boards are then put in a vise as shown. Start the bit with the screw point in the fold, using a 1-in. bit, and bore a hole ½ in. deep. When the cardboard is taken from the vise it will appear as shown at B and when unfolded, as at A.

HOW TO CARRY BOOKS

Almost all school children carry their books with a strap put around and buckled very tight. This will make dents in the cover where the board overlaps the body of the book. If the strap is left loose, the books are liable to slip out. Place the cover of one book between the cover and fly leaf of its neighbor and the difficulty will be remedied. This will place the books in alternate directions. Books stacked

in this manner do not require the strap buckled tight, or, they can be carried without any strap just as well.—Contributed by Thos. De Loof, Grand Rapids, Mich.

HOW TO CHAIN A DOG

A good way to chain a dog and give him plenty of ground for exercise is to stretch a clothesline of a galvanized wire between the house and barn on which is placed a ring large enough to slide freely. The chain from the dog's collar is fastened to the ring. This method can also be used for tethering a cow or horse, the advantage being the use of a short tie rope eliminating the possibility of the animal becoming entangled.

The Dog Has Plenty of Room for Exercise

HOW TO FIND THE BLIND SPOT IN THE EYE

Make a small black circular dot ½ in. in diameter on a piece of cardboard and about 3 in. from the center of this dot draw a star. Hold the cardboard so that the star will be directly in front of one eye, while the dot will be in front of the other. If the star is in front of the left eye, close the right eye and look steadily at the star while you move the cardboard until the point is reached where the dot disappears. This will prove the presence of a blind spot in a person's eye. The other eye can be given the same experiment by turning the cardboard end for end. The blind spot does not indicate diseased eyes, but it simply marks the point where the optic nerve enters the eyeball, which point is not provided with the necessary visual end organs of the sight, known as rods and cones.

A wax from the rafie palm of Madagascar is being used as a substitute for beeswax.

How to Fit Corks

Occasionally odd-sized bottles are received in stores which require corks cut to fit them. No matter how sharp a knife may be, it will leave some sharp edges after cutting the cork, which will cause leakage. The illustration shows three very effective methods of reducing the size of corks. The one shown in Fig. 1 is made from two pieced of ½-in. wood fastened together at one end with a common hinge. Two or three grooves are cut cross-wise in sizes desired. The cork is put into the groove and both pieces are pressed together, which will make the cork smaller.

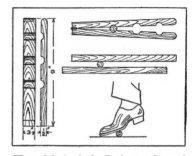

Three Methods for Reducing Size of Corks

Rolling the cork between two flat surfaces (Fig. 2) is simple and almost as good as pressing in the grooves. A cork rolled on the floor (Fig. 3) is a quick and effective way. A slower and equally as good way is to soak the cork in hot water for a short time.—Contributed by L. Szerlip, Brooklyn, N. Y.

Standing at the cylinder end and looking toward the fly-wheel of an engine, the wheel will be at the right if the engine is right-hand.

How to Hang Your Hat on a Lead Pencil

Take a smooth hexagon lead pencil, one without either rubber or metal end, and place it against a door or window casing; then with a firm, heavy pressure slide the pencil some 3 or 4 in. and it will stay as if glued to the casing. You may now hang your hat on the end of the pencil.

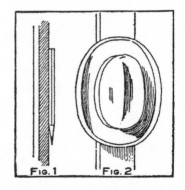

When you slide the pencil along the casing, do it without any apparent effort, and it will appear to your audience as thought you had hypnotized it. This is a very neat trick if performed right. Figure 1 shows the pencil on the casing and Fig. 2 the hat hanging on it.

HOW TO HOLD A SCREW ON A SCREWDRIVER

A screw that is taken from a place almost inaccessible with the fingers requires considerable patience to return it with an ordinary screwdriver unless some holding-on device is used. I have found that by putting a piece of cardboard or thick paper with the blade of the screwdriver in the screw head slot, the screw may be held and turned into places that it would be impossible with the screwdriver alone.—Contributed by C. Chatland, Ogden, Utah.

HOW TO MAKE A PAPER BOOK COVER

Book covers become soiled in handling and especially school books. Various methods are applied for making a temporary cover that will protect the book cover. A paper cover can be quickly made by using a piece of paper larger than both covers on the book when they are open. Fold the paper on the long dotted line, as shown in Fig. 1. When the folds are made the paper should then be just as wide as the book cover is high. The ends are then folded on the short dotted lines, which will make it appear as shown in Fig. 2. The paper thus folded is placed on the book cover as shown in Fig. 3—Contributed by C. E. McKinney, Jr., Newark, N. J.

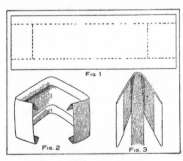

To Protect Book Covers

HOW TO MAKE JAPANESE PORTIERES

These very useful and ornamental draperies can be easily made at home by anyone possessing a little ingenuity. They can be made of various materials, the most durable being bamboo, although beads of glass or rolled paper will produce good results. Substances such as straw, while readily adaptable and having a neat appearance, are less durable and will quickly show wear. The paper beads are easily made, as shown in Figs. 1, 2 and 3. In Figs. 1 and 2 are shown how the paper is cut tapering, and as it appears after rolling and gluing down the ends. A straight paper bead is shown in Fig. 3.

The first step is to select the kind of beads desired for stringing and then procure the hanging cord. Be sure to get a cord of such size that the beads will slip on readily and yet have the least possible lateral movement. This is important to secure neatness. One end of each cord is tied to a leather strap. Iron or brass rings can be used if desired.

Cut all the cords the same length, making allowance for the number of knots necessary to produce the design selected. Some designs require only one knot at the bottom. It is best to make a rough sketch of the design on paper. This will greatly aid the maker carrying on the work.

When the main part of the screen is finished, the cross cords, used for spacing and binding the whole together, are put in place. This is done with a needle made from a piece of small wire, as shown in Fig. 4.

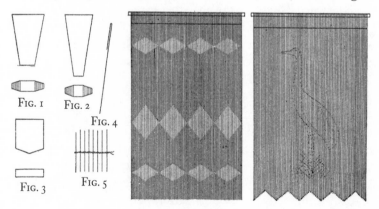

FIG. 1   FIG. 2

FIG. 4

FIG. 3   FIG. 5

Bamboo and Straw Portieres

The cross cords are woven in as shown in Fig. 5. As many of these cross cords can be put in as desired, and if placed from 6 to 12 in. apart, a solid screen will be made instead of a portiere. The twisted cross cords should be of such material, and put through in such manner that they will not be readily seen. If paper beads are used they can be colored to suit and hardened by varnishing.

The first design shown is for using bamboo. The cords are knotted to hold the bamboo pieces in place. The finished portière will resemble drawn work in cloth. Many beautiful hangings can be easily fashioned.

The second design is to be constructed with a plain ground of either straw, bamboo or rolled paper. The cords are hung upon a round stick with rings of metal to make the sliding easy.

The design is made by stringing beads of colored glass at the right ished portiere will resemble drawn work in cloth. Many beautiful hangings can be easily fashioned.

The second design is to be constructed with a plain ground of either straw, bamboo or rolled paper. The cords are hung upon a round stick with rings of metal to make the sliding easy.

The design is made by stringing beads of colored glass at the right places between the lengths of ground material. One bead is placed at the extreme end of each cord. The rows of twisted cord placed at the top keep the strings properly spaced.— Contributed by Geo. M. Harrer, Lockport, N. Y.

HOW TO REMOVE PAPER FROM STAMPS

Old stamps as they are purchased usually have a part of the envelope from which they are taken sticking to them and in removing this paper many valuable stamps that are stuck to pieces of envelopes in hot water and in a short time they can be separated without injury. Dry the stamps between in this way will have a much better appearance when placed in an album.—Contributed by L. Szerlip, Brooklyn, N. Y.

How to Waterproof Canvas

The method used by the British navy yards for waterproofing and painting canvas so it will not become stiff and cracked is as follow: One ounce of yellow soap and ½ pt. of hot water are mixed with every 7 lb. of paint to be used. The mixture is applied to the canvas with a brush. This is allowed to dry for two days and then a coat of the same paint, without the soap, is laid on. When this last coat is dry the canvas may be painted any color desired. After three days of drying the canvas may be folded up without sticking together, and is, of course, waterproof. Canvas waterproofed in this manner makes an excellent covering for portable canoes and canvas boats. The color mixture for the soap and second application is made from 1 lb. of lampblack and 6 lb. of yellow ocher, both in oil; the finish coat may be any color desired. When no paint is to be used on the canvas it may be waterproofed with a mixture made from soft soap dissolved in hot water, and a solution of iron sulphate added. Iron sulphate, or ferrous sulphate, is the green vitriol. The vitriol combines with the potash of the soap, and the iron oxide is precipitated with the fatty acid as insoluble iron soap. This precipitate is then washed, dried and mixed with linseed oil.

Killing Mice and Rats

A simple and inexpensive means for killing mice and rats is to leave yeast cakes lying around where they can eat them.—Contributed by Maud McKee, Erie, Pa.

Key Card for Writing Unreadable Post Cards

A key card for use in correspondence on postals that makes the matter unreadable unless the recipient has a duplicate key card is made as follows: Rule two cards the size of postal, one for the sender and one for the receiver, dividing them into quarters. These quarters are subsequently divided into any convenient number of rectangular parts—six in this case.

These parts are numbered from one to six in each quarter beginning at the outside corners and following in the same order in each quarter. Cut out one rectangle of each number with a sharp knife, distributing them over the whole card. Then put a prominent figure 1 at the top of one side, 2 at the bottom and 3 and 4 on the other side. The numbering and the cutouts are shown in Fig. 1. The two key cards are made alike.

The key card is used by placing it over a postal with the figure 1 at the top and writing in the spaces from left to right as usual, Fig. 3, then put 2 at the top, Fig. 4, and proceed as before, then 3 as in Fig. 5, and 4 as in Fig. 6. The result will be a jumble of words as shown in Fig. 2, which cannot be read to make any sense except by use of a key card.—Contributed by W. J. Morey, Chicago.

LINES AND LETTERS MADE WITH A CARPENTER'S PENCIL

The sketch shows some unusual work made with a carpenter's pencil. If the flat lead is notched with a three-cornered file (Fig. 1), two parallel lines may be drawn at one stroke, or various rulings may be made, as shown in Fig. 2. Broad lines can be made, as shown in Fig. 3, or unequal widths as in Fig. 4. In Figs. 2, 5 and 6 are shown lines especially adapted for the book-keeper or draftsman. If one lacks the ability to draw old English letters with a pen, the letters may be first drawn with a carpenter's pencil (Fig. 7) and the outlines marked with ink and finally filled in. Narrow lines are made with points cut as in Figs. 8 and 9. A little practice with the carpenter's pencil in making these letters will enable the student to finally produce them with the pen used for the purpose.

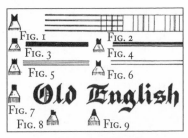

Pencil Points and Their Work

	4	4	1
2	5	5	
	6	6	3
3	6		3
2		5	2
1	4.		1

READ	YOURSELF	WRITTEN	THE
WORLD	SO	POSTED	POPULAR
MECHANICS	ON	YOU	IN
CAN	SCIENCE	MAGAZINE	THE
PROGRESS	TO	AND	UNDERSTAND
IT	MECHANICS	KEEP	OF

READ   1.   POPULAR   MECHANICS   MAGAZINE   TO   KEEP   2

YOURSELF 2   POSTED   ON   THE   PROGRESS   1   OF

3.   THE   WORLD   IN   SCIENCE   AND   MECHANICS

4. WRITTEN   SO   YOU   CAN   UNDERSTAND   IT   C

The Key Card

MAKING COINS STICK TO WOOD BY VACUUM

Take a quarter and place it flat against a vertical surface of wood such as the side of a bookcase, door facing or door panel, and strike it hard with a downward sliding motion, pressing it against the wood. Take the hand

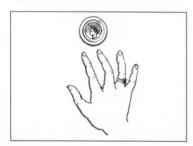

away and the coin will remain on the woodwork. The striking and pressure expel the air between the quarter and the wood, thus forming a vacuum sufficient to hold the coin.

NEW WAY TO REMOVE A BOTTLE STOPPER

Take a bottle of liquid, something that is carbonated, and with the aid of a napkin form a pad which is applied to the lower end of the bottle. Strike hard with repeated blows against the solid surface of a wall, as shown in the sketch, and the cork will be driven out, sometimes with so much force that a part of the liquid comes

Removing the Stopper

with it and deluges the spectators, if desired by the operator.

PERFUME-MAKING OUTFIT

The real perfume from the flowers is not always contained in the liquid purchased for perfume. The most expensive perfume can be made at home for less than 10 cents an ounce. The outfit necessary is a large bottle or glass jar with a smaller bottle to fit snugly into the open mouth of the large one. Secure a small piece of very fine sponge and wash it clean to thoroughly remove all grit and sand. Saturate the sponge with pure olive oil, do not use strong oil, and place it inside of the smaller bottle.

Fill the large bottle or jar with flowers, such as roses, carnations, pansies, honeysuckles or any flower having a strong and sweet odor. Place the small bottle containing the sponge upside down in the large one, as shown in the illustration.

The bottle is now placed in the sun and kept there for a day and then the flowers are removed and fresh ones put in. Change the flowers each day as long as they bloom. Remove the sponge and squeeze out the oil. For each drop of oil add 2 oz. of grain alcohol. If stronger perfume is desired add only 1 oz. alcohol to each drop of oil.

REMOVING A TIGHT-FITTING RING FROM A FINGER

When a ring cannot be removed easily from the finger, take a string or thread and draw one end through between the ring and the flesh. Coil the other end of the string around the finger covering the part from the ring to and over the finger joint. Uncoil the string by taking the end placed through the ring and at the same time keep the ring close up to the string. In this way the ring can be easily slipped over the knuckle and off from the finger.—Contributed by J. K. Miller, Marietta, Penn.

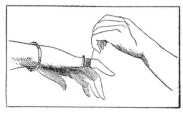

Wrapping the Finger

REMOVING OLD PAINT

A chair more than a hundred years old came to me by inheritance. It was originally painted green and had been given two coats of dark paint or varnish within the last 30 years. Desiring to improve the appearance of the relic, I decided to remove the paint and give it a mahogany stain. The usual paint removers would readily take off the two latter coats but had no effect upon the first. I tried to remove the troublesome green in various ways, but with little success until I applied a hot, saturated solution of concentrated lye. By coating the paint with this repeatedly, applying one coat upon another for two days, and

then using a stiff brush, the layer was easily and completely removed.—Contributed by Thos. R. Baker, Chicago, Ill.

REPAIRING CRACKED GRAMOPHONE RECORDS

Some time ago I received two gramophone records that were cracked in shipment but the parts were held together with the paper label. As these were single-faced disk records, I used the following method to stick them together: I covered the back of one with shellac and laid the two back to back centering the holes with the crack in one running at right angles to the crack in the other. These were placed on a flat surface and a weight set on them. After several hours' drying, I cleaned the surplus shellac out of the holes and played them.

As the needle passed over the cracks the noise was hardly audible. These records have been played for a year and they sound almost as good as new.—Contributed by Marion P. Wheeler, Greenleaf, Oregon.

SOFTENING LEATHER IN GLOVES AND BOOTS

The leather in high-top boots and gauntlet gloves may be softened and made waterproof by the use of plain mutton tallow. Apply hot and rub in well with the fingers.

STICKING A COIN AGAINST THE WALL

Cut a small notch in a coin—ten-cent piece or quarter will do—so a small point will project. When this is pressed firmly against a wood casing or partition the coin will stick tightly.

THE BUTTONED CORD

Cut a piece of heavy paper in the shape shown in Fig. 1 and make two cuts down the center and a slit as long as the two cuts are wide at a point about 1 in., below them. A string is put through the slit, the long cuts and back through the slit and then a button is fastened to each end. The small slit should not be so large as the buttons. The trick is to remove the string. The solution is quite simple. Fold the paper in the middle and the part between the long cuts will form a loop. Bend this loop down and pass it through the small slit. Turn the paper around and it will appear as shown in Fig. 2. One of the buttons may now be drawn through and the paper restored to its original shape.

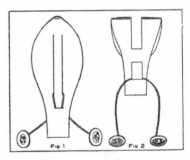

Removing the String

TO HANG HEAVY THINGS ON A NAIL

Boys will find many places around the house, where a hook to hang things on will be a great convenience. Instead of buying hooks use wire nails, and if driven as shown in the cut, they will support very heavy weights. Drive the lower nail first.

To Preserve Putty

Putty, when left exposed to the air, will soon become dry and useless. I have kept putty in good condition for more than a year by placing it in a glass jar and keeping it entirely covered with water.

Turning Lights On and Off from Any Number of Places

This can be done by the use of any number of reversing switches such as those shown at B and C. These are inserted between the two-way switches A and D. Turning such a switch up or down connects the four contact pieces either diagonally as at C, or lengthwise as at B. The diagram shows connection from A to D, when the lamps will be on, but by turning either of these four switches into its alternative position, shown by the dotted lines, the circuit will be broken and the lights extinguished. When this has been done, the circuit may be restored and the lamps lighted again by altering either of the four switches in exactly the same way, and so on.

It will be observed that a reversing switch used in this way practically undoes whatever is done by the other switches. In the accompanying diagram only two reversing switches are shown and the lights can be independently controlled from four distinct positions. Any number of reversing switches can be placed between the two-way switches A and D to increase the number of place from which the lights could be turned on and off.—Contributed by J. S. Dow, Mayfield, London.

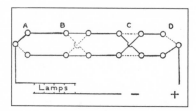

Wiring Diagram

WATERPROOFING A WALL

The best way to make a tinted wall waterproof is to first use a material composed of cement properly tinted and with no glue in it—one that will not require a glue size on the wall. After this coating of cement is applied directly to the plaster, cover it completely with water enamel and, when dry, give the surface a thorough coating of varnish. This will make a perfectly impervious covering, which steam, water or heat will not affect.—Contributed by Julia A. White, New York City.

DROPPING COINS IN A GLASS FULL OF WATER

Take a glass and fill it to the brim with water, taking care that the surface of the water is raised a little above the edge of the glass, but not running over. Place a number of nickels or dimes on the table near the glass and ask your spectators how many coins can be put into the water without making it overflow. No doubt the reply will be that the water will run over before two coins are dropped in. But it is possible to put in ten or twelve

of them. With a great deal of care the coins may be made to fall without disturbing the water, the surface of which will be come more and more convex before the water overflows.

A BOOKMARK

A very handy bookmark can be made by attaching a narrow ribbon to an ordinary paper clip and using it as shown in the sketch. The clip is slipped over the binding in the back of the book as shown in the sketch.—Contributed by Chester E. Warner, Kalamazoo, Mich.

PAPER-CLIP BOOKMARK

The combination of a paper clip and a calling card makes a good bookmark. The clip and card can be kept together by piercing the card and bending the ends of the wire to stick through the holes. The clip is attached to a page as shown in the sketch.—Contributed by Thos. DeLoof, Grand Rapids, Mich.

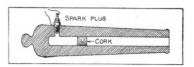

Gas Cannon Loaded

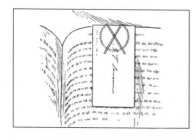

A Gas Cannon

If you have a small cannon with a bore of 1 or 1½ in., bore out the fuse hole large enough to tap and fit in a small sized spark plug such as used on a gasoline engine. Fill the cannon with gas from a gas jet and then push a cork in the bore close up to the spark plug. Connect one of the wires from a battery to a spark coil and then to the spark plug. Attach the other wire to the cannon near the spark plug. Turn the switch to make a spark and a loud report wall follow. Contributed by Cyril Tegner, Cleveland, O.

A Home-Made Elderberry Huller

As we had only one day to pick elderberries, we wanted to get as many of them as we could in that time. We could pick them faster than they could be hulled by hand so we made a huller to take along with us to hull the berries as fast as they were picked. We procured a box and made a frame, Fig. 1, to fit it easily, then made another frame the same size and put a piece of wire mesh between them as shown in Fig. 2, allowing a small portion of the mesh to stick out of the frames. The top frame would keep the berries from rolling or jumping off, and the bottom frame kept the wire mesh and frame from being shaken off the box. The projecting edges of the mesh would keep the frame on the top edge of the box. The top view of the frame is shown in Fig. 1 and the end in Fig. 5, and the box on which the frame

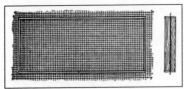

Frame With Wire　　　End
FIG. 1　　　　　　FIG. 5

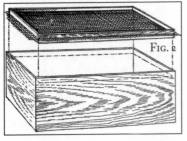

FIG. 2

FIG. 3

rests in Fig. 3. The actual size of the wire mesh used is shown in Fig. 4. One person could hull with this huller as many berries as two persons would pick.—Contributed by Albert Niemann, Pittsburg, Pa.

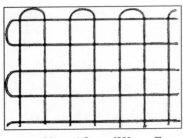

Natural Size of Wire　　FIG. 4
Details of the Elderberry Huller

A WINDOW DISPLAY

A novel and attractive aeroplane window display can be easily made in the following manner: Each aeroplane is cut from folded paper, as shown in the sketch, and the wings bent out on the dotted lines. The folded part in the center is pasted together. Each aeroplane is fastened with a small thread from the point A as shown. A figure of an airman can be pasted to each aeroplane. One or more of the aeroplanes can be fastened in the blast of an electric fan and kept in flight the same as a kite. The fan can be concealed to make the display more real. When making the display, have the background of such a color as to conceal the small threads holding the aeroplanes.—Contributed by Frederick Hennighausen, Baltimore, Md.

Paper Aeroplanes in Draft

SPORTS AND GAMES

A Wrestling Mat

The cost of a wrestling mat is so great that few small clubs can afford to own one. As we

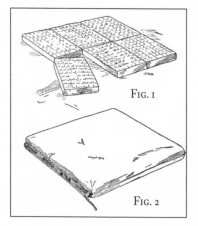

Fig. 1

Fig. 2

Made of Bed Mattresses

did not see our way clear to purchase such a mat, I made one of six used bed mattresses (Fig. 1) purchased from a second-hand dealer. I ordered a canvas bag,

12 ft. 3 in. by 12 ft. 9 in., from a tent company, to cover the mattresses. The bag consisted of two pieces with the seam along each edge. The mattresses were laid side by side and end to end and the bag placed on and laced up as shown in Fig. 2.—Contributed by Walter W. White, Denver, Colo.

Home-Made Roller Skates

The rubber-tired wheels of an old carpet sweeper can be used to advantage in making a pair of roller skates. In Fig. 1 is shown how an iron washer

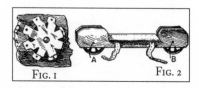

Fig. 1

Fig. 2

Rubber Tired Roller Skate

or two may be fastened to the wood with a piece of sheet metal to support the short axles of the wheels. The wheels are oiled through the holes A and B, Fig. 2. These holes should be smaller than the axles. The two side pieces are fastened together with a board nailed on the top edges, as shown. This board also furnishes the flat top for the shoe sole. Two straps are attached for fastening the skate to the shoe.—Contributed by Thos. De Loof, Grand Rapids, Mich.

How To Make a Water Bicycle

Water bicycles afford fine sport, and, like many another device boys make, can be made of material often cast off by their people as rubbish. The principal material necessary for the construction of a water

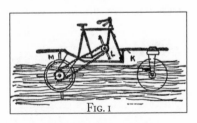

Fig. 1

Water Bicycle Complete

bicycle is oil barrels. Flour barrels will not do—they are not strong enough, nor can they be made perfectly airtight. The grocer can furnish you with oil barrels at a very small cost, probably let you have them for making a few deliveries for him. Three barrels are required for the water bicycle, although it can be made with but two. Figure 1 shows the method of arranging the barrels; after the manner of bicycle wheels.

Procure an old bicycle frame and make for it a board platform about 3 ft. wide at the rear end and tapering to about 2 ft. at the front, using cleats to hold the board frame, as shown at the shaded portion K. The construction of the barrel part is shown in Fig. 2. Bore holes in the center of the heads of the two rear barrels and also in the heads of the first barrel and put a shaft of wood through the rear barrels and one through the front barrel, adjusting the side pieces to the shafts, as indicated.

Next place the platform of the bicycle frame and connections thereon. Going back to Fig. 1 we see that the driving chain passes from the sprocket

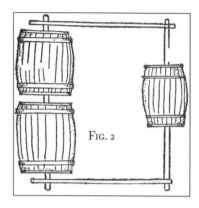

Fig. 2

Barrel Float for Bicycle

The speed is slow at first, but increases as the force is generated and as one becomes familiar with the working of the affair. There is no danger, as the airtight barrels cannot possibly sink.

Another mode of putting together the set of barrels, using one large one in the rear and a small one in the front is presented in Fig. 3. These two barrels are empty oil barrels like the others. The head holes are bored and the proper wooden shafts are inserted and the entrance to the bores closed tight by calking with hemp and putty or clay. The ends of the shafts turn in the wooden frame where the required bores are made to receive the same. If the journals thus made are well oiled, there will not be much friction. Such a frame can be fitted with a platform and a raft to suit one's

driver L of the bicycle frame to the place downward between the slits in the platform to the driven sprocket on the shaft between the two barrels. Thus a center drive is made. The rear barrels are fitted with paddles as at M, consisting of four pieces of board nailed and cleated about the circumference of the barrels, as shown in Fig. 1.

The new craft is now ready for a first voyage. To propel it, seat yourself on the bicycle seat, feet on the pedals, just as you would were you on a bicycle out in the street. The steering is effected by simply bending the body to the right or left, which causes the craft to dip to the inclined side and the affair turns in the dipped direction.

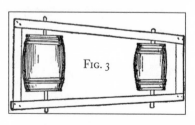

Fig. 3

Another Type of Float

individual fancy built upon it, which can be paddled about with ease and safety on any pond. A sail can be rigged up by using a mast and some sheeting; or even a little houseboat, which will give any amount of pleasure, can be built.

How to Make Skating Shoes

Remove the clamp part, as shown in Fig. 1, from an ordinary clamp skate. Drill holes in the top part of the skate for screws. Purchase a pair of high shoes with heavy soles and fasten the skates to the soles with screws, as shown in Fig. 2. When completed the skating shoes will have the appearance shown on Fig. 3. These will make as good skating shoes as can be purchased, and very

much cheaper.—Contributed by Wallace C. Newton, Leominster, Mass.

How to Make Weights for Athletes

Many times boys would like to make their own shots and weights for athletic stunts, but do not know how to go about it to cast the metal. In making a lead sphere as shown in the illustration, it is not necessary to know the method of molding. The round lead weight for shot-putting or hammerthrowing can be cast in a hollow cardboard or pressed-paper ball, sold in department and toy stores for 10 cents. Cut a ½-in. hole in the ball as shown in Fig. 1 and place it with the hole up in damp sand and press or tamp the sand lightly around the ball as shown in the section, Fig. 2. Cover over about 1 in. deep. A wood plug

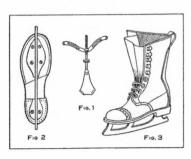

Skating Shoes

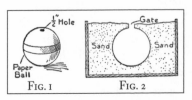

Mold for the Lead

inserted in the hole will prevent any sand falling inside. When the sand is tamped in and the plug removed, it leaves a gate for the metal. Pour melted lead into the gate until it is full, then, when cool, shake it out from the sand and remove the charred paper. A file can be used to remove any rough places. The dry paper ball prevents any sputtering of the hot lead.—Contributed by W. A. Jaquythe, Richmond, Cal.

WIRE TERMINALS FOR BATTERY CONNECTIONS

Good connections on the end of wires for batteries can be made from cotter pins, Fig. 1, about 1½ in. long. Each end of the wire is put through the eye of a cotter pin, twisted around itself and soldered. The connection and eye are then covered with tape as shown in Fig. 2.

When connecting to batteries, spread the pin and push the parts under the nut with one part on each side of the binding-post. When the nuts are tightened the connection will be better than with the bare wire.—Contributed by Howard S. Bott.

A CHECKER BOARD PUZZLE

Place eight checker men upon the checker board as shown in the first row in the sketch. The puzzle is to get them in four piles of two men each without omitting to jump over two checker men every time a move is made.

The first move is to jump 5 over 4 and 3 on 2 which is

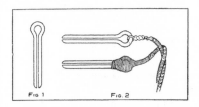

Cotter Pin Wire Terminals

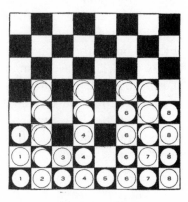

Placing the Checkers

shown in the second row, then jump 3 over 4 and 6 on 7 and the positions will appear as shown in the third row; jump 1 over 2 and 5 on 4 to get the men placed like the fourth row and the last move is to jump 8 over 3 and 7 on 6 which will make the four piles of two men each as shown in the fifth row.— Contributed by I. G. Bayley, Cape May Point, N. J.

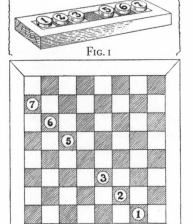

Fig. 1

Fig. 2

Position of the Men

A Checker Puzzle

Cut a block from a board about 3 in. wide and 10 in. long. Sandpaper all the surfaces and round the edges slightly. Mark out seven 1-in. squares on the surface to be used for the top and color the squares alternately white and black. Make six men by sawing a curtain roller into pieces about ⅜ in. thick. Number the pieces 1, 2, 3, 5, 6 and 7, and place them as shown in Fig. 1. The puzzle is to make the first three change places with the last three and move only one at a time. This may be done as follows:

Move 1—Move No. 3 to the center.

Move 2—Jump No. 5 over No. 3.

Move 3—Move No. 6 to No. 5's place.

Move 4—Jump No. 3 over No. 6.

Move 5—Jump No. 2 over No. 5.

Move 6—Move No. 1 to No. 2's place.

Move 7—Jump No. 5 over No. 1.

Move 8—Jump No. 6 over No. 2.

Move 9—Jump No. 7 over No. 3.

Move 10—Move No. 3 into No. 7's place.

Move 11—Jump No. 2 over No. 7.

Move 12—Jump No. 1 over No. 6.

Move 13—Move No. 6 into No. 2's place.

Move 14—Jump No. 7 over No. 1.

Move 15—Move No. 1 into No. 5's place.

After the 15 moves are made the men will have changed places. This can be done on a checker board, as shown in Fig. 2, using checkers for men, but be sure you so situate the men that they will occupy a row containing only 7 spaces.— Contributed by W. L. Woolson, Cape May Point, N. J.

Covering railroad signals with gold leaf has taken the place of painting on some roads. Gold leaf will stand the wear of the weather for 15 or 20 years, while paint requires recovering three or four times a year.

A DOVETAIL JOINT PUZZLE

A simple but very ingenious example in joinery is illustrated. In the finished piece, Fig. 1, the dovetail appears on each side of the square stick of wood, the illustration, of course, shows only two sides, the other two are identical. The joint is separable and each part is solid and of one piece. In making, take two pieces of wood, preferably of contrasting colors, such as cherry and walnut or mahogany and boxwood, about 1½ in. square and of any length

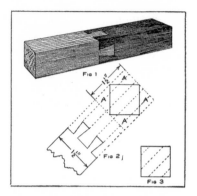

How the Joint Is Cut

desired. Cut the dovetail on one end of each stick as shown in Fig. 2, drive together and then plane off the triangular corners marked A. The end of each piece after the dovetails are cut appear as shown in Fig. 3, the lines marking the path of the dovetail through the stick.

Pure rain water is the best to use in a cooling system of an automobile engine, as it is free from the mineral substances which are deposited in the radiator, piping and jackets by hard water.

A MERRY-GO-ROUND THRILLER

As a home mechanic with a fondness for amusing the children I have seen many descriptions of merry-go-rounds, but never one which required so little material, labor and time, and which gave such satisfactory results, as the one illustrated herewith. It was erected in our back yard one afternoon, the materials being furnished by an accommodating lumber pile, and a little junk, and it has provided unlimited pleasure for "joyriders," little and big, from all over the neighborhood. It looks like a toy, but once seat yourself in it and begin to go around. and, no matter what your age or size may be, you will have in a minute enough thrill and excitement to last the balance of the day.

The illustration largely explains itself, but a few dimensions will be a help to anyone wishing to construct the apparatus. The upright is

Swinging on the Merry-Go-Round

a 4 by 4-in. timber, set 3 ft. in the ground with 8 ft. extending above. It is braced on four sides with pieces 2 in. square and 2 ft. long, butting against short stakes. The upper end of the post is wound with a few rounds of wire or an iron strap to prevent splitting. The cross-piece is 2 in. square, 12 ft. long, strengthened by a piece 4 in. square and 5 ft. long. These two pieces must be securely bolted or spiked together. A malleable iron bolt, ¾ in. in diameter and 15 in. long is the pivot. On this depends the safety of the contrivance, so it must be strong enough, and long enough to keep firmly in the post. Drive this bolt in a ⅜-in. hole bored in the post, which will make it a sufficiently tight fit. Make the hole for the bolt very loose through the cross-piece, so that there will be plenty of "wobble," as this is one of the mirth-making features of the machine. Use a heavy washer at the head. The seats are regular swing boards, supported by a stout and serviceable rope. A ¾-in. rope is not too heavy. One set of ropes are passed through holes at the end of the crosspiece and knotted on top. The other set should be provided with loops at the top and slid over the crosspiece, being held in position by spikes as shown. This makes an easy adjustment. Seat the heavier of the riders on the latter seat, moving it toward the center until a balance with the lighter rider is reached. A rope tied to the crosspiece about 2 ft. from the center, for the "motive power" to grasp, completes the merry-go-round.

Put plenty of soap or grease between the crosspiece and upright. Be sure to have room for the ropes to swing out at high speed, with no trees or buildings in the way. The "wobble" mentioned will give an agreeable undulating motion, which adds greatly to the flying sensation. This will be found surprisingly evident for so small a machine. As there is no bracing, care must be taken to have the two riders sit at the same moment, or the iron bolt will be bent out of line. If it is to be used for adults, strong clear material only should be employed.— Contributed by C. W. Nieman.

An Aid in Sketching

Sketching requires some little training, but with the apparatus here illustrated an inexperienced person can obtain excellent results. The apparatus is made of a box 8 in. deep, 8 in. wide and about 1 ft. long. A double convex lens, G, is fitted in a brass tube which should have a sliding fit in another shorter and larger tube fastened to the end of the box. A mirror, H, is set at an angle of 45 deg. in the opposite end of the box. This reflects the rays of light passing through the lens to the surface K, which may be either of ground or plain glass. The lid or cover E F protects the glass and keeps the strong light out when sketching. The inside of the box and brass tube are painted a dull black.

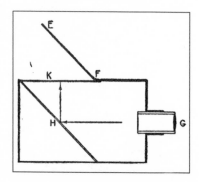

In use, the device is set with the lens tube directed toward the scene to be painted or sketched and the lens focused so the reflected picture will be seen in sharp detail on the glass. Select your colors and put them on the respective colors depicted on the glass. If you wish to make a pencil drawing, all you have to do is to fill in the lines in the picture on the ground glass. If a plain glass is used, place tracing paper on its surface, and the picture can be drawn as described.

An Austrian Top

All parts of the top are of wood and they are simply to make. The handle is a piece of pine, 5¼ in. long, 1¼ in. wide and ¾ in. thick. A handle, ¾ in. in diameter, is formed on one end, allowing only 1¼ in. of the other end to remain rectangular in shape. Bore a ¾-in. hole

in this end for the top. A ¹⁄₁₆-in. hole is bored in the edge top enter the large hole as shown. The top can be cut from a broom handle or a round stick of hardwood.

To spin the top, take a piece of stout cord about 2 ft. long, pass one end through the ¹⁄₁₆-in. hole and wind it on the small part of the top in the usual way, starting at the bottom and winding upward. When the shank is covered, set the top in the ¾-in. hole. Take hold of the handle with the left hand and the end of the cord with the right hand, give a good quick pull on the cord and the top will jump clear of the handle and spin vigorously.—Contributed by J. F. Tholl, Ypsilanti, Michigan.

Attaching Runners to a Bicycle for Winter Use

Instead of storing away your bicycle for the winter, attach runners and use it on the ice. The runners can be made from ¼-in. by 1-in. iron and fastened to the bicycle frame as shown in the sketch. The tire is removed from the rim of the rear wheel

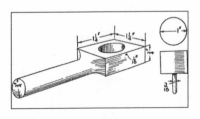

Parts of the Tip

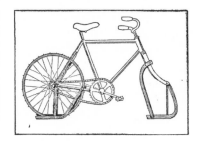

Bicycle Fitted with Runners for Snow

and large screws turned into the rim, leaving the greater part of the screw extending. Cut off the heads of the screws and file them to a point. The rear runners should be set so the rim of the wheel will be about ½ in. above the runner level.—Contributed by C. R. Welsh, Manhattan, Kan.

DEVICE FOR BASEBALL THROWING PRACTICE

Anyone training to be a baseball player will find the device shown in the accompanying illustration a great help when practicing alone. It consists of two cement slabs, one flat and upright, the other curved and on the ground. The vertical slab is fastened securely against a fence, barn or shed. The barn or the shed is preferable, for if the slab is fastened to a fence, the ball will bound over a great many times and much time will be lost in finding it.

The player stands as far as he cares from the slabs and throws the ball against the lower slab. The ball immediately rebounds to the upright slab and returns with almost as great a force as it was delivered. If the thrower does not throw the ball exactly in the same spot each time, the ball will not rebound to the same place, consequently the eye and muscles are trained to act quickly, especially if the player stands within 15 or 20 ft. of the slabs and throws the ball with great force.

This apparatus also teaches a person to throw accurately, as a difference in aim of a few inches on the lower slab may cause

Ball Bounding on Concrete Slabs

the ball to fly away over the player's head on the rebound.— Contributed by F. L. Oilar, La Fayette, Indiana.

HOW TO MAKE A GLIDER

BY CARL BATES

A gliding machine is a motorless aeroplane, or flying-machine, propelled by gravity and designed to carry a passenger through the air from a high point to a lower point some distance away. Flying in a glider is simply coasting down hill on the air, and is the most interesting and exciting sport imaginable. The style of glider described in this article is known as the "two-surface" or "double-decked" aeroplane, and is composed of two arched cloth surfaces placed one above the other.

In building a glider the wood material used should be straight-grained spruce, free from knots. First prepare from spruce planks the following strips of wood. Four long beams ¾ in. thick, 1¼ in. wide and 20 ft. long; 12 cross-pieces ¾ in. thick, ¾ in. wide and 3 ft. long; 12 uprights ½ in. thick, 1½ in.

wide and 4 ft long; 41 strips for the bent ribs ³⁄₁₆ in. thick, ½ in. wide and 4 ft. long; 2 arm sticks 1 in. thick, 2 in. wide and 3 ft. long; the rudder sticks ¾ in. square and 8 ft long; several strips ½ in. by ¾ in. for building the vertical and horizontal rudders. The frames for the two main surfaces should be constructed first, by bolting the crosspieces to the long beams at the places shown by the dimensions in Fig. 1. If 20-ft. lumber cannot be procured, use 10-ft. lengths and splice them, as shown in Fig. 3. All bolts used should be ⅛ in. in diameter and fitted with washers on both ends. These frames formed by the crosspieces should be braced by diagonal wires as shown. All wiring is done with No. 16 piano wire.

The 41 ribs may be nailed to the main frames on the upper side by using fine flat-headed brads ⅞ in. long. These ribs are spaced 1 ft. apart and extend 1 ft. beyond the rear edges of the main frames, as shown in Fig. 1. After nailing one end of a rib to the front long beam, the rib is arched by springing down the loose end and nailing to the rear beam. The ribs should have a curve as shown in Fig. 2, the amount of curvature being the same in all the ribs.

The frames of the main surfaces are now ready to be covered with cloth. Cambric or bleached muslin should be used for the covering, which is tacked to the front edge, stretched tightly over the bent ribs and fastened securely with tacks to the rear ends of the ribs. The cloth should also be glued to the ribs for safety. In the center of the lower plane surface there should be an opening 2 ft. wide and 4 ft. long for the body of the operator. Place the two main surfaces 4 ft. apart and connect with the 12 uprights, placed in the corner of each crosspiece and beam. The uprights are fastened by bolting to the crosspieces, as shown in Fig. 2. The whole structure is made strong and rigid by bracing with diagonal wires, both laterally and longitudinally.

The vertical rudder is to keep the machine headed into the wind and is not movable. This rudder is made of cloth stretched over a light wooden frame, which is nailed to the rudder sticks connecting to the main frame. The horizontal rudder is also made of cloth stretched over a light wooden frame, and arranged to intersect the vertical rudder at its center. This rudder is held in position and strengthened by diagonal wires and guy wires. The horizontal rudder is also immovable, and its function is to prevent the machine from diving, and also to keep it steady in its flight. The rudders are fastened to the glider by the two rudder sticks, and these sticks are held rigid by diagonal wires and also by guy wires leading to the sides of the main frames as shown in Fig. 1. The two arm sticks should be spaced about 13 in. apart and bolted to the long beams in the center of the opening in the lower plane where the operator is to take his position.

The glider should be examined to see that the frame is not warped or twisted. The surfaces must be true or the machine will be hard to balance when in flight. To make a glide, take the glider to the top of a hill, get in between the arm sticks are under the arms as shown, run

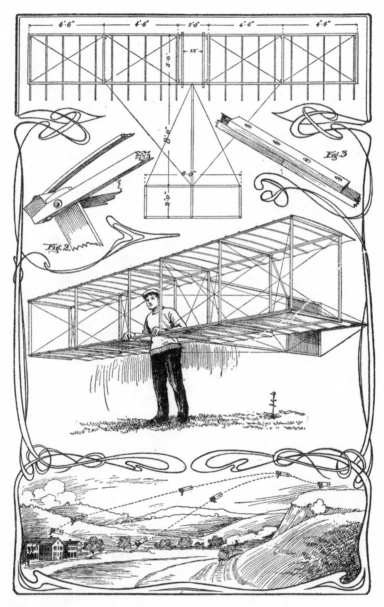

Details of the Glider

a few steps against the wind and leap from the ground. You will find that the machine has a surprising amount of lift, and if the weight of the body is in the right place you will go shooting down the hillside in free flight. The landing is made by pushing the weight of the body backwards. This will cause the glider to tip up in front, slacken speed and settle. The operator can then land safely and gently on his feet. Of course, the beginner should learn by taking short jumps, gradually increasing the distance as he gains skill and experience in balancing and landing.

The proper position of the body is slightly ahead of the center of the planes, but this must be found by experience. The machine should not be used in winds blowing faster than 15 miles an hour. Glides are always made against the wind, and the balancing is done by moving the legs. The higher the starting point the farther one may fly. Great care should be exercised in making landings, otherwise the operator might suffer a sprained ankle or perhaps a broken limb. The

illustration shows two line of flight from a hilltop, the glider travels on the upper line caused by the body of the operator taking a position a little back of the proper place, and on the lower line he changes his position from front to back while flying, which causes the dip in the line.

HOW TO MAKE A LEAD PENCIL RHEOSTAT

Take an ordinary lead pencil and cut seven notches at equal intervals on the pencil down to and around the lead, leaving it bare. A seven-point switch is constructed on a board of suitable size making the points by using screws that will go through the board. A small piece of tin or brass will do for a switch and is fastened as shown.

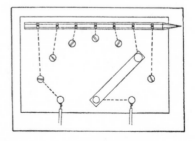

Simple Rheostat

The connections are made on the back side of the board as shown by the dotted lines. This will reduce 40 to 50 volts down to 5 or 10 volts for short lengths of time.—Contributed by Roy Newby, San Jose, Cal.

HOW TO MAKE A LIFE BUOY

Any boy may be able to make for himself or friends a life buoy for emergency use in a rowboat or for learning to swim.

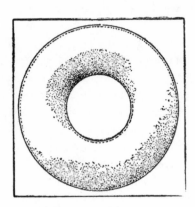

Purchase 1¾ yd. of 30-in. canvas and cut two circular pieces 30 in. in diameter, also cutting a round hole in the center of them 14 in. in diameter. These two pieces are sewed together on the outer and inner edges, leaving a space about 12 in. in length unsewed on the outer seam. Secure some of the cork used in packing Malaga grapes from a grocery or confectionery store and pack it into the pocket formed between the seams through the hole left in the outer edge. When packed full and tight sew up the remaining space in the seam. Paint the outside surface and the seams well with white paint to make it watertight.—Contributed by Will Hare, Petrolea, Ont.

HOW TO MAKE A PADDLE BOAT

A rowboat has several disadvantages. The operation of the oars is both tiresome and uninteresting, and the oarsman is obliged to travel backward. By replacing the oars with paddles, as show in the illustration, the operator can see where he is going and enjoy the exercise much better than with oars. He can easily steer the boat with his

Paddle Boat in Operation

feet, by means of a pivoted stick in the bottom of the boat, connected by cords to the rudder.

At the blacksmith shop have a ⅝-in. shaft made, as shown at A, Fig. 2. It will be necessary to furnish a sketch giving all the dimensions of the shaft, which should be designed to suit the dimensions of the boat, taking care that sufficient clearance is allowed, so that the cranks in revolving will not strike the operator's knees. If desired, split-wood handles may be placed on the cranks, to prevent them from rubbing the hands.

The bearings, B, may be made of hardwood, but preferably of iron pipe filled with melted babbitt. If Babbitt is used, either thoroughly smoke or chalk the shaft or wrap paper around it to prevent the babbitt sticking. The pieces of pipe may be then fastened to the boat by means of small pipe straps, such as may be obtained at any plumber's at a very small cost.

The hubs, C, should be made of wood, drilled to fig the shaft and mortised out to hold the paddles, D. The covers, E, may be constructed of thin wood or galvanized iron and should be braced by triangular boards, as shown in Fig. 1. If galvanized iron is used, it should be exposed to the weather two or three months before painting, or the paint will come off, spoiling its appearance.

SIMPLY MADE WIRE PUZZLE

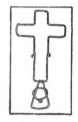

The object of the simply made wire puzzle is to get the ring off, which is not easy unless you know how. To do so it is necessary to move the triangle with ring to one of the hinge joints and fold the puzzle. Then slip the ring of the triangle over the hinge joint and it will slip all around and off at the other hinge.

Diabolo is pronounced Dee-ab-lo.

THE NORWEGIAN SKI

You have often read of the ski, the snowshoe used by the Norwegians and other people living in the far north. With them the men and women glide down the snow-covered

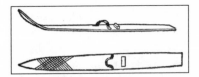

Home-Made Skis

mountain sides, leap across ditches, run races and have all kinds of sport. They are just as amusing to the American boy who has ever learned to manipulate them, and it is wonderful how much skill can be attained in their use. Any boy with a little mechanical ingenuity can make a pair of skis (pronounced skees). They can be made from two barrel staves. Select staves of straight grained wood. Sharpen the ends of each and score each end by cutting grooves in the wood, as shown in the cut, Fig. 7. A pocket knife or small gouge will suffice for this work. Then smear the end of the staves with oil and hold them close to a hot fire until they can be bent so as to tip the toes upward, as shown in the picture, Fig. 7. Then with a cord bind the staves as they are bent and permit them to remain thus tied until they retain the curved form of their own accord. Now screw on top of each ski a little block, just broad and high enough to fit in front of the heels of your shoe. Fasten a strap in front of each block through which to slip your toes, and the skis are made. The inside of the shoe hell should press firmly against the block and the toe be held tightly under the strap. This will keep the skis on your feet. Now procure a stick with which to steer and hunt a snow bank. At first you will afford more amusement to onlookers than to yourself, for the skis have a way of trying to run in opposite directions, crosswise and various ways, but with practice you will soon become expert in their manipulation.

THE ROLLING MARBLE

Take a marble and place it on a smooth surface, the top of a table will do. Ask some one to cross their first and second fingers and place them on the marble as

shown in the illustration. Then have the person roll the marble about and at the same eyes or look in another direction. The person will imagine that there are two marbles instead of one.

How to Attach a Sail to a Bicycle

This attachment was constructed for use on a bicycle to be ridden on the well packed sands of a beach, but it could be used on a smooth, level road as well. The illustration shows the main frame to consist of two boards, each about 16 ft. long, bent in the shape of a boat, to give plenty of room for turning the front wheel. On this main frame is built up a triangular mast, to carry the mainsail and jib, having a combined area of about 40 sq. ft. The frame is fastened to the bicycle by numerous pieces of rope.

Sailing on a bicycle is very much different from sailing in a boat, for the bicycle leans up against the wind, instead of heeling over with it as the boat. It takes some time to learn the supporting power of the wind, and the angle at which one must ride makes it appear that a fall is almost sure to result. A turn must be made by turning out of the wind, instead of, as in ordinary sailing, into it; the boom supporting the bottom of the mainsail is then swung over to the opposite tack, when one is traveling at a good speed.

Bicycle Sailing on a Beach

TOYS

A Tailless Kite

The frame of a 3-ft. kite is made of two sticks, each 3 ft. long. These are tied together so that the cross stick will be at a distance of 15 per cent of the full length of the upright stick, from its end, or in this case 5.4 in. The sticks may be made straight-grained pine, ⅜ in. square, for small kites, and larger hardwood sticks, for larger kites.

The cross stick is bent into a bow by tying a strong cord across from end to end. The center of the bend should be 4½ in. above the ends. The bend is shown in the sketch. Connect all four ends or points with a cord, being careful not to pull the bend of the cross stick down, but seeing that it remains straight across the kite. When this is done the frame is ready for the cover.

The cover will require 2½ sheets of tissue paper, 20 by 30 in., which should be pasted together as the sketch indicates. Cut out the paper, allowing 2 in. margin for lapping over the cord on the frame. Place the frame on the cover with the convex side toward the paper and paste the margin over the cord, allowing the paper to bag a little to form pockets for the air to lift the kite. The corners should be reinforced with

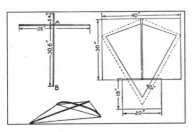

Plan and Dimensions for Kite

144

circular pieces of paper pasted over the ends of the sticks.

The flying cord is attached to the points A and B of the frame. There is no cross cord. The kite will fly at right angles to the flying from the ground by laying it with the head toward the operator and pulling it up into the wind.—Contributed by Chas. B. Damik, Cooperstown, N. Y.

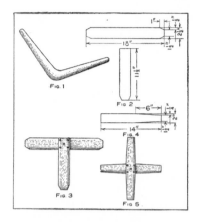

Details of Three Boomerangs

BOOMERANGS AND HOW TO MAKE THEM

A boomerang is a weapon invented and used by the native Australians, who seemed to have the least intelligence of any race of mankind. The boomerang is a curved stick of hardwood, Fig. 1, about ⁵⁄₁₆ in. thick, 2½ in. wide and 2 ft. long, flat on one side, with the ends and the other side rounding. One end of the stick is grasped in one hand with the convex edge forward and the flat side up and thrown upward. After going some distance and ascending slowly to a great height in the air with a quick rotary motion, it suddenly returns in an elliptical orbit to a spot near the starting point. If thrown down

on the ground the boomerang rebounds in a straight line, pursuing a ricochet motion until the object is struck at which it was thrown.

Two other types of boomerangs are illustrated herewith and they can be made as described. The materials necessary for the T-shaped boomerang are: One piece of hard maple ⁵⁄₁₆ in. thick, 2½ in. wide, and 3 ft. long; five ½-in. flatheaded screws. Cut the piece of hard maple into two pieces, one 11½ in. and the other 18 in. long. The corners are cut from these pieces as shown in Fig. 2, taking care to cut exactly the same amount from each corner. Bevel both sides of the pieces, making the edges very thin so they will cut the air better. Find the exact center of the long piece and make a line 1¼ in. on each side of the center and fasten the short length between the lines with the screws as shown in Fig. 3. The short piece should be fastened perfectly square and at right angles to the long one.

The materials necessary for the cross-shaped boomerang are one piece hard maple ⁵⁄₁₆ in. thick, 2 in. wide and 30 in. long and five ½-in. flat-headed screws. Cut the maple into two 14-in. pieces and plane the edges of these pieces so the ends will be 1½ in. wide, as shown in Fig. 4. Bevel these pieces the same as the ones for the T-shaped boomerang. The two pieces are fastened together as shown in Fig. 5. All of the boomerangs when completed should be given several coats of linseed oil and thoroughly dried. This will keep the wood from absorbing water and becoming heavy. The last two boomerangs are thrown in a similar way to the first one, except that one of the pieces is grasped in the hand and the throw given with a quick underhand motion. A little practice is all that is necessary for one to become skillful in throwing them.—Contributed by O. E. Tronnes, Wilmette, Ill.

HOME-MADE BOY'S CAR

The accompanying cut shows how a boy may construct his own auto car. The car consists of parts used from a boy's wagon and some old bicycle parts. The propelling device is made by using the hanger, with all its parts, from a bicycle. A part of the bicycle frame is left attached to the hanger and is fastened to the main board of the car by blocks of wood as shown. The chain of a bicycle is used to connect the crank hanger sprocket to a small sprocket fastened in the middle of the rear axle of the

Boys' Home-Made Auto

car. The front axle is fastened to a square block of wood, which is pivoted to the main board. Ropes are attached to the front axle and to the back part of the main board to be used with the feet in steering the car. To propel the auto, turn the cranks by taking hold of the bicycle pedals.—Contributed by Anders Neilsen, Oakland, Cal.

How to Discharge a Toy Cannon by Electricity

A device for discharging a toy cannon by electricity can be easily made by using three or four dry batteries, a switch and a small induction coil capable of giving a ⅛-in. spark. Fasten a piece of wood, A, to the cannon, by means of machine screws or, if there are no trunnions on the cannon, the wood may be made in the shape of a ring and slipped on over the muzzle. The fuse hole of the cannon is counterbored as shown and a small hole is drilled at one side to receive a small piece of copper wire, E. The wood screw, C, nearly touches E and is connected to one binding post of the induction coil. The other binding post is connected with the wood screw, D, which conducts the current into the cannon, and also holds the pieces of wood, A and B, in position.

When the cannon is loaded, a small quantity of powder is placed in the counterbore, and the spark between C and E ignites this and discharges the cannon. A cannon may be fired from a distance in this way, and as there is no danger of any spark remaining after the current is shut off, it is safer than the ordinary cannon which is fired by means of a fuse.—Contributed by Henry Peck, Big Rapids, Mich.

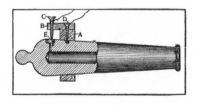

Electrical Attachment for
Discharging Toy Cannon

How to Make a Box Kite

As some of the readers of Amateur Mechanics may desire to build a box kite, a simple method of constructing one

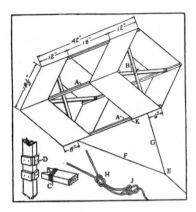

Detail of Box Kite

of the modern type is given in detail as follows: The sticks should be made of straight-grained wood, which may be either spruce, basswood or white pine. The longitudinal corner spines, A A, should be ⅜ in. square by 42 in. long, and the four diagonal struts, B, should be ¼ in. by ½ in., and about 26 in. long. Two cloth bands should be made to the exact dimensions given in the sketch and fastened to the four longitudinal sticks with 1-oz. tacks. It is well to mark the positions of the sticks on the cloth bands, either with a soft lead-pencil or crayon, in order to have the four sides of each band exactly equal. The ends of the bands should be lapped over at least ½ in. and sewed double to give extra strength, and the edges should be carefully hemmed, making the width, when finished, exactly 12 in. Probably the best cloth for this purpose is nainsook, although lonsdale cambric or lightweight percaline will answer nearly as well.

The diagonal struts, B, should be cut a little too long, so that they will be slightly bowed when put in position, thus holding the cloth out taut and flat. They should be tied together at the points of intersection and the ends should be wound with coarse harnessmaker's thread, as shown at C, to prevent splitting. The small guards, D, are nailed or glued to the longitudinal sticks to prevent the struts slipping out of position. Of course the ends of the struts could be fastened to the longitudinal strips if desired, but if made as described the kite may be readily taken apart and rolled up for convenience in carrying.

The bridle knots, E, are shown in detail at H and J. H is a square knot, which may be easily loosened and shifted to a different position on the bridle, thus adjusting the lengths of F and G. A bowline knot should be tied at J, as shown, to prevent slipping. If the kite is used in a light wind, loosen the square knot and shift nearer to G, thus shortening G and lengthening F, and if a strong wind is blowing, shift toward F, thereby lengthening G and making F shorter. In a very strong wind do not use the bridle, but fasten a string securely to the stick at K.—Contributed by Edw. E. Harbert, Chicago.

An experienced photographer uses blacklead for grooves about a camera or holder. A small quantity is rubbed well into the grooves and on the edges of shutters, that refuse to slide easily, with gratifying results. Care must be taken to allow no dust to settle in the holders, however.

How to Make a Crossbow and Arrow Sling

It the making of this crossbow it is best to use maple for the stock, but if this wood cannot be procured, good straight-grained pine will do. The material must be 1½ in. thick, 6 in. wide and a trifle over 3 ft. long. The bow is made from straight-grained oak, ash, or hickory, ⅝ in. thick, 1 in. wide and 3 ft. long. A piece of oak, ⅜ in. thick, 1½ in. wide and 6 ft. long, will be sufficient to make the trigger, spring and arrows. A piece of tin, some nails and a good cord will complete the materials necessary to make the crossbow.

The piece of maple or pine selected for the stock must be planed and sandpapered on both sides, and then marked and cut as shown in Fig. 1. A groove is cut for the arrows in the top straight edge ⅜ in. wide and ⅜ in. deep. The tin is bent and fastened on the wood at the back end of the groove where the cord slips out of the notch; this is to keep the edges from splitting.

A mortise is cut for the bow at a point 9½ in. from the end of the stock, and one for the trigger 12 in. from the opposite end, which should be slanting a little as shown by the dotted lines. A spring, Fig. 2, is made from a good piece of oak and fastened to the stock with

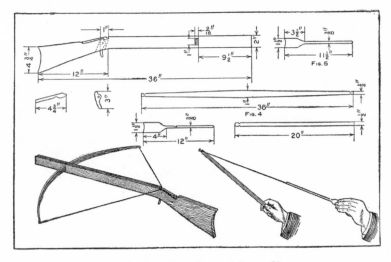

Details of the Bow-Gun and Arrow Sling

two screws. The trigger, Fig. 3, which is ¼ in. thick, is inserted in the mortise in the position when pulled back, and adjusted so as to raise the spring to the proper height, and then a pin is put through both stock and trigger, having the latter swing quite freely. When the trigger is pulled, it lifts the spring up, which in turn lifts the cord off the tin notch.

The stick for the bow, Fig. 4, is dressed down from a point ¾ in. on each side of the center line to ½ in. wide at each end. Notches are cut in the ends for the cord. The bow is not fastened in the stock, it is wrapped with a piece of canvas 1½ in. wide on the center line to make a tight fit in the mortise. A stout cord is now tied in the notches cut in the ends of the bow making the cord taut when the wood is straight.

The design of the arrows is shown in Fig. 5 and they are made with the blades much thinner than the round part.

To shoot the crossbow, pull the cord back and down in the notch as shown in Fig. 6, place the arrow in the groove, sight and pull the trigger as in shooting an ordinary gun.

The arrow sling is made from a branch of ash about ½ in. in diameter, the bark removed and a notch cut in one end, as shown in Fig. 7. A stout cord about 2½ ft. long is tied in the notch and a large knot made in the other or loose end. The arrows are practically the same as those used on the crossbow, with the exception of a small notch which is cut in them as shown in Fig. 8.

To throw the arrow, insert the cord near the knot in the notch of the arrow, then grasping the stick with the right hand and holding the wing of the arrow with the left, as shown in Fig. 9, throw the arrow with a quick slinging motion. The arrow may be thrown several hundred feet after a little practice.—Contributed by O. E. Trownes, Wilmette, Ill.

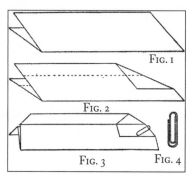

Folding the Paper

HOW TO MAKE A PAPER AEROPLANE

A very interesting and instructive toy aeroplane can be made as shown in the accompanying illustrations. A sheet of paper is first folded, Fig. 1, then the corners on one end are doubled over, Fig. 2, and the whole piece finished up and held together with a paper clip as in Fig. 3. The paper clip to be used should be like the one shown in Fig. 4. If one of these clips is not at hand, form a piece of wire in the same shape, as it will be needed for balancing purposes as well as for holding the paper together. Grasp the aeroplane between the thumb and fore-finger at the place marked A in Fig. 3, keeping the paper as level as possible and throwing it as you would a dart. The aeroplane will make an easy and graceful flight in a room where no air will strike it.—Contributed by J. H. Crawford, Schenectady, N. Y.

HOW TO MAKE A PAPER BOAT

A Light Boat That Can Be Easily Carried

Now you might think it absurd to advise making a paper boat, but it is not, and you will find it in some respects and for some purposes better than the wooden boat. When it is completed you will have a canoe, probably equal to the Indian's bark canoe. Not only will it serve as an ideal fishing boat, but when you want to combine hunting and fishing you can put your boat on your shoulders and carry it from place to place wherever you want to go and at the same time carry your gun in your hand. The material used in its construction is inexpensive and can be purchased for a few dollars.

Make a frame (Fig. 1 on which to stretch the paper. A board 1 in. thick and about 1 ft. wide and 11½ ft. long is used for a keel, or backbone, and is cut tapering for about a third of its length, toward each end, and beveled on the outer edges (A, Fig. 2) The cross-boards (B, B, Fig. 2) are next sawed from a pine board 1 in. thick. Shape these as shown by A, Fig. 4, 13 in. wide by 26 in. long, and cut away in the center to avoid useless weight. Fasten them cross-wise to the bottom-board as shown in Fig. 1 and 2, with long stout screws, so as to divide the keel into three nearly equal parts. Then add the stem and stern pieces (C, C, Fig. 2). These are better, probably, when made of green elm. Screw the pieces to the bottom-board and bend them, as shown in Fig. 2,

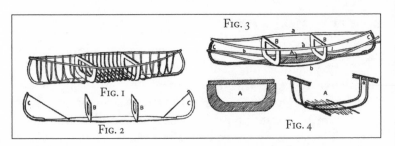

Details of Framework Construction

by means of a string or wire, fastened to a nail driven into the bottom. Any tough, light wood that is not easily broken when bending will do. Green wood is preferable, because it will retain the shape in which it has been bent better after drying. For the gunwales (a, a, Fig. 3), procure at a carriage factory, or other place, some light strips of ash, ⅜ in. thick. Nail them to the cross-boards and fasten to the end pieces (C, C,) in notches, by several wrappings of annealed iron wire or copper wire, as shown in Fig. 3. Copper wire is better because it is less apt to rust. For fastening the gunwales to the crossboards use nails instead of screws, because the nails are not apt to loosen and come out. The ribs, which are easily made of long, slender switches of osier willow, or similar material, are next put in, but before doing this, two strips of wood (b, b, Fig. 3) should be bent and placed as in Fig. 3. They are used only temporarily as a guide in putting in the ribs, and are not fastened, the elasticity of the wood being sufficient to cause them to retain their position.

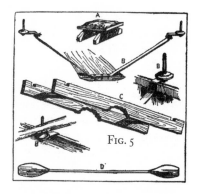

Fig. 5

Important Features of Construction

The osiers may average a little more than ½ in. in thickness and should be cut, stripped of leaves and bark and put in place while green and fresh. They are attached to the bottom by means of shingle nails driven through holes previously made in them with an awl, and are then bent down until they touch the strips of ash (b, b, Fig. 3), and finally cut off even with the tops of the gunwales, and notched at the end to receive them (B, Fig. 4). Between the cross-boards the ribs are placed at intervals of 2 or 3 in., while in other parts they are as much as 5 or 6 in. apart. The ribs having all been fastened in place as described, the loose strips of ash (b, b, Fig. 3) are withdrawn and the framework will appear somewhat as in Fig. 1. In order to make all firm and to prevent the ribs from changing position, as they are apt to do, buy some split cane or rattan, such as is used for making chair-bottoms, and, after soaking it in water for a short time to render it soft and pliable, wind it tightly around the gunwales and ribs where they join, and also interweave it among the ribs in other places, winding it about them and forming an irregular network over the whole frame. Osiers probably make the best ribs, but twigs of some other trees, such as hazei or birch, will answer nearly as well. For the ribs near the middle of the boat, twigs 5 or 6 ft. long are required. It is often quite difficult to get these of sufficient thickness throughout, and so, in such cases, two twigs may be used to make one rib, fastening the butts side by side on the bottom-board, and the smaller ends to the gunwales, as before described. In drying, the rattan becomes very tight and the twigs hard and stiff.

The frame-work is now complete and ready to be covered. For this purpose buy about 18 yd. of very strong wrapping-paper. It should be smooth on the surface, and very tough, but neither stiff nor very thick. Being made in long rolls, it can be obtained in almost any length desired. If the paper be 1 yd. wide, it will require about two breadths to reach around the frame in the widest part. Cut enough of the roll to cover the frame and then soak it for a few minutes in water. Then turn the frame upside down and fasten the edges of the two strips of paper to it, by lapping them carefully on the under side of the bottom-board and tacking them to it so that the paper hangs down loosely on all sides. The paper is then trimmed, lapped and doubled over as smoothly as possible at the ends of the frame, and held in place by means of small clamps. It should be drawn tight along the edges, trimmed and doubled down over the gunwale, where it is firmly held by slipping the strips of ash (b, b) just inside of the gunwales into notches which should have been cut at the ends of the cross-boards. The shrinkage caused by the drying will stretch the paper tightly over the framework. When thoroughly dry, varnish inside and out with asphaltum varnish thinned with turpentine, and as soon as that has soaked in, apply a second coat of the same varnish, but with less turpentine; and finally cover the laps or joints of the paper with pieces of muslin stuck on with thick varnish. Now remove the loose strips of ash and put on another layer of paper, fastening it along the edge of the boat by replacing the strips as before. When the paper is dry, cover the laps with muslin as was done with the first covering. Then varnish the whole outside of the boat several times until it presents a smooth shining surface. Then take some of the split rattan and, after wetting it, wind it firmly around both gunwales and inside strip, passing it through small holes punched in the paper just below the gunwale, until the inside and outside strips are bound together into one strong gunwale. Then put a piece of oil-cloth in the boat between the cross-boards, tacking it to the bottom-board. This is done to protect the bottom of the boat.

Now you may already have a canoe that is perfectly watertight, and steady in the water, if it has been properly constructed of good material. If not, however, in a few days you may be disappointed to find that it is becoming leaky. Then the best remedy is to cover the whole boat with unbleached muslin, sewed at the ends and tacked along the gunwales. Then tighten it by shrinking and finally give it at least three coats of a mixture of varnish and paint. This will doubtless stop the leaking entirely and

Off for a Hunt

will add but little to either the weight or cost.

Rig the boat with wooden or iron rowlocks (B, B, Fig. 5), preferably iron, and light oars. You may put in several extra thwarts or cross-sticks, fore and aft, and make a movable seat (A, Fig. 5.) With this you will doubtless find your boat so satisfactory that you will make no more changes.

For carrying the boat it is convenient to make a sort of short yoke (C, Fig, 5), which brings all the weight upon the shoulders, and thus lightens the labor and makes it very handy to carry.

HOW TO MAKE AND FLY A CHINESE KITE

The Chinese boy is not satisfied with simply holding the end of a kite string and running up and down the block or field trying⁻ to raise a heavy paper kite with a half pound of rags for a tail. He makes a kite as light as possible without any tail which has the peculiar property of being able to move in every direction. Sometimes an expert can make one of these

kites travel across the wind for several hundred feet; in fact, I have seen boys a full block apart bring their kites together and engage in a combat until one of their kites floated away with a broken string, or was punctured by the swift dives of the other, and sent to earth, a wreck.

The Chinese boy makes his kite as follows:

From a sheet of thin but tough tissue paper about 20 in. square, which he folds and cuts along the dotted line, as shown in Fig. 1, he gets a perfectly square kite having all the properties of a good flyer, light and strong. He shapes two pieces of bamboo, one for the backbone and one for the bow. The backbone is flat, ¼ by 3⁄32 in. and 18 in. long. This he smears along one side with common boiled rice. Boiled rice is one of the best adhesives for use on paper that can be obtained and the Chinese have used it for centuries while we are just waking up to the fact that it makes fine photo paste. Having placed the backbone in position, paste two triangular pieces of paper over the ends of the stick to prevent tearing. The bow is now bent,

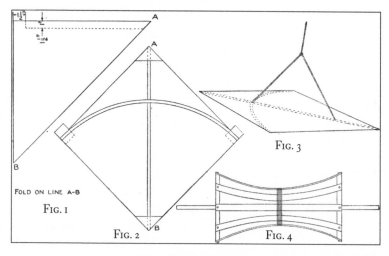

FOLD ON LINE A-B

FIG. 1

FIG. 2

FIG. 3

FIG. 4

Parts of a Chinese Kite

and the lugs extending from the sides of the square paper are bent over the ends of the bow and pasted down. If the rice is quite dry or mealy it can be smeared on and will dry almost immediately, therefore no strings are needed to hold the bow bent while the paste dries.

After the sticks are in position the kite will appear as shown in Fig. 2. The dotted lines show the lugs bent over the ends of the bow and pasted down. Figure 3 shows how the band is put on and how the kite is balanced. This is the most important part and cannot be explained very well. This must be done by experimenting and it is enough to say that the kite must balance perfectly. The string is fastened by a slip-knot to the band and moved back and forth until the kite flies properly, then it is securely fastened.

A reel is next made. Two ends—the bottoms of two small peach baskets will do— are fastened to a dowel stick or broom handle, if nothing better is at hand. These ends are placed about 14 in. apart and strips nailed between them as shown in Fig. 4, and the centers drawn in and bound with a string. The kite string used is generally a heavy packing thread. This is run through a thin flour or rice paste until it is thoroughly coated, then it is run through a quantity of crushed glass. The glass should be beaten up fine and run through a fine sieve to make it about the same as No. 2 emery. The particles should be extremely sharp and full of splinters. These particles adhere to the pasted string and when dry are so sharp that it cannot be handled without scratching the fingers, therefore the kite is flown entirely from the reel. To wind the string upon the reel, all that is necessary is to lay one end of the reel stick in the bend of the left arm and twirl the other end between the fingers of the right hand.

A Chinese boy will be flying a gaily colored little kite from the roof of a house (if it be in one of the large cities where they have flat-roofed houses) and a second boy will appear on the roof of another house perhaps 200 ft. away. Both have large reels full of string, often several hundred yards of it. The first hundred feet or so is glass-covered string, the balance common packing thread,

or glass-covered string. As soon as the second boy has his kite aloft, he begins maneuvering to drive it across the wind and over to the first kite. First, he pays out a large amount of string, then as the kite wabbles to one side with its nose pointing toward the first kite, he tightens his line and commences a steady quick pull. If properly done his kite crosses over to the other and above it. The string is now payed out until the second kite is hanging over the first one's line. The wind now tends to take the second kite back to its parallel and in so doing makes a turn about the first kite's string. If the second kite is close enough, the first tries to spear him by swift dives. The second boy in the meantime is see-sawing his string and presently the first kite's string is cut and it drifts away.

It is not considered sport to haul the other fellow's kite down as might be done and therefore a very interesting battle is often witnessed when the experts clash their kites.— Contributed by S. C. Bunker, Brooklyn, N. Y.

How to Make Boomerangs

When the ice is too thin for skating and the snow is not right for skis, about the only thing to do is to stay in the house. A boomerang club will help to fill in between and also furnishes good exercise for the muscles of the arm. A boomerang can be made of a piece of well seasoned hickory plank. The plank is well steamed in a wash boiler or other large kettle and then bent to a nice curve, as shown in Fig. 1. It is held in this curve until dry, with two pieces nailed on the sides as shown.

After the piece is thoroughly dried out, remove the side pieces and cut it into sections with a saw, as shown in Fig. 2. The pieces are then dressed round. A piece of plank 12 in. wide and 2 ft. long will make six boomerangs.

To throw a boomerang, grasp it and hold the same as a club, with the hollow side away from you. Practice first at some object about 25 ft. distant, and in a short time the thrower will be able to hit the mark over 100 ft. away. Any worker in wood can turn out a great number of boomerangs cheaply.—Contributed by J. E. Noble, Toronto, Ontario.

Imitation Arms and Armor—Part II

Imitation swords, stilettos and battleaxes, put up as ornaments, will look well if they are arranged on a shield which is hung high up on a wall of a room or hall, says the English Mechanic, London. The following described arms are authentic designs of the original articles. A German sword of the fifteenth century is shown in Fig. 1. This sword is 4 ft. long with the crossguard and blade of steel. The imitation sword is made of wood and covered with tinfoil to produce the steel color. The shape of the sword is marked out on a piece of wood that is about ⅛ in. thick with the aid of a straightedge and pencil, allowing a little extra length

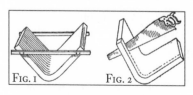

Bending and Cutting the Wood

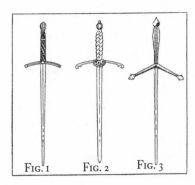

Fig. 1   Fig. 2   Fig. 3

Three Fifteenth Century Swords

on which to fasten the handle. Cut the sword out with a saw and make both edges thin like a knife blade and smooth up with sandpaper. The extra length for the handle is cut about 1 in. in width and 2 in. long. The handle is next carved and a mortise cut in one end to receive the handle end of the blade. As the handle is to represent copper, the ornamentations can be built up of wire, string, small rope and round-headed nails, the whole finally having a thin coat of glue worked over it with a stiff bristle brush and finished with bronze paint.

The crossbar is flat and about 1 in. in width. Cut this out of a piece of wood and make a center hole to fit over the extra length on the blade, glue and

put it in place. Fill the hole in the handle with glue and put it on the blade. When the glue is thoroughly dry, remove all the surplus with a sharp knife. Sheets of tinfoil are secured for covering the blade. Cut two strips of tinfoil, one about ½ in. wider than the blade and the other ¼ in. narrower. Quickly cover one side of the blade with a thin coat of glue and evenly lay on and press down the narrow strip of tinfoil. Stick the wider strip on the other side in the same way, allowing equal margin of tinfoil to overlap the edges of the blade. Glue the overlapping edges and press them around on the surface of the narrow strip. The crossguard must be covered in the same manner as the blade. When the whole is quite dry, wipe the blade up and down several times with light strokes using a soft rag.

The sword shown in Fig. 2 is a two-handed Swiss sword about 4 ft. in length, sharp on both edges with a handle of dark wood around which is wound spirally a heavy piece of brass or copper wire and held in place with round-headed brass nails. The blade and crossbar are in imitation steel. The projecting ornament in the center of the crossguard may be cut from heavy pasteboard and bent into shape, then glued on the blade as shown.

In Fig. 3 is shown a claymore, or Scottish sword of the fifteenth century. This sword is about 4 ft. long and has a wood handle bound closely around with heavy cord. The crossbar and blade are steel, with both edges sharp. A German poniard is shown in Fig. 4. This weapon is about 1 ft. long, very broad, with wire or string bound handle, sharp edges on both sides. Another poniard of the fourteenth century is shown in Fig. 5. This weapon is also about 1 ft. long with wood handle and steel embossed blade. A sixteenth century German poniard is shown in Fig. 6. The blade and ornamental crossbar is of steel, with both edges of the blade sharp. The handle is of wood. A German stiletto, sometimes called cuirass breakers, is shown in Fig. 7. This stiletto has a wood handle, steel crossbar and blade of steel with both edges sharp.

In Fig. 8 is shown a short-handled flail, which is about 2½ ft. long with a dark handle of wood, studded with brass or steel nails. A steel band is placed around the handle near the top. The imitation of the steel band is made by gluing a piece of tinfoil on a strip of cardboard and tacking it to the handle. A large screweye is screwed into the top of the handle. The spiked ball may be made of wood or clay. Cover the ball with some pieces of linen, firmly glued on. When dry, paint it a dark brown or black. A large screweye must be inserted in this ball, the same as used on the end of the handle, and both eyes connected with a small piece of rope twisted into shape. The rope is finished by covering with tinfoil. Some short and heavy spike-headed nails are driven into the ball to give it the appearance shown in the illustration.

A Russian knout is shown in Fig. 9. The lower half of the handle is of wood, the upper part iron or steel, which can be imitated by covering a piece of wood that is properly shaped with tinfoil. The whole handle can be made of wood in one piece, the lower part painted black and the upper part covered with tinfoil. A screweye is screwed into the upper end. A length of real iron or steel chain is used to connect the handle with the ball. The ball is made as described in Fig. 8. The spikes in the ball are about 1 in. in length. These must be cut from pieces of wood, leaving a small peg at the end and in the center about the size of a No. 20 spike. The pegs are glued and inserted into holes drilled into the ball.

In Fig. 10 is shown a Sclavonic horseman's battle-axe which has a handle of wood painted dark gray or light brown; the axe is of steel. The blade is cut from a piece of ¼-in. wood with a keyhole saw. The round part is made thin and sharp on the edge. The thick hammer side of the axe is built up to the necessary thickness to cover the handle by gluing on pieces of wood the same thickness as used for the blade, and gradually shaping off to the middle of the axe by the use of a chisel, finishing with sandpaper and covering with tinfoil. Three large, round-headed brass or iron nails fixed into the front side of the handle will complete the axe.

At the beginning of the sixteenth century horseman's battle-axes shaped as shown in Fig. 11 were used. Both handle and axe are of steel. This axe is made similar to the one described in Fig. 10. When the woodwork is finished the handle and axe are covered with tinfoil.

IMITATION ARMS AND ARMOR—PART VI

A mass of any kind of clay that is easily modeled and fairly stiff must be prepared and kept moist and well kneaded for making the models over which paper is formed to make the shape of the articles illustrated in these sketches. A modeling

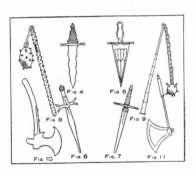

Ancient Weapons

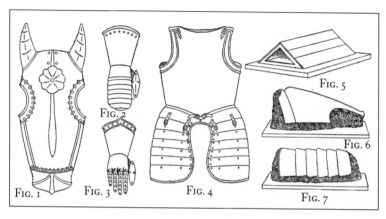

Armor and Clay Models

board must be made of one large board or several pieces joined closely together upon which to work the clay, says the English Mechanic, London. The size of the board depends upon the size of the work to be made.

An open chamfron of the fifteenth century is shown in Fig. 1. This piece of horse armor, which was used in front of a horse's head, makes a splendid center for a shield on which are fixed the swords, etc., and is a good piece for the amateur armorer to try his hand on in the way of modeling in clay or papier maché work. The opening for the animal to put his head into is semicircular, and the sides do not cover the jaws. As the main part of this armor is worn in front of the head the extreme depth is about 4 in. The entire head piece must be modeled in clay with the hands, after which it is covered with a thin and even coating of sweet or pure olive oil. A day before making the clay model some pieces of thin, brown wrapping paper are torn in irregular shapes to the size of the palm of the hand and put to soak in a basin of water in which a table-spoonful of size has been dissolved. If size cannot be obtained from your local painter, a weak solution of glue will do equally well. All being ready, and the clay model oiled, take up one piece of paper at a time and very carefully place it on the surface of the model, pressing it on well and into and around any crevices and patterns. Continue this operation until the clay model is completely covered on every part. This being done, give the paper a thin and even coating of glue, which must be quite hot and laid on as quickly as possible. Lay on a second layer of paper as carefully as before, then another coat of glue, and so on until there are five or six coats of glue and paper. When this is dry it will be strong enough for all ornamental purposes. The ragged edges of the paper are trimmed off with a sharp knife and the whole surface smoothed with fine sandpaper. Then carefully glue on sections of tinfoil to give the armor the appearance of steel. The armor is now removed from the model.

A mitten gauntlet of the fifteenth century is shown in Fig. 2. This can be made in one piece, with the exception of the thumb shield, which is separate. The thumb shield is attached to the thumb of an old glove which is fastened with round headed nails on the inside of the gauntlet. The part covering the wrist is a circular piece, but the back is not necessary as it would not be seen when the gauntlet is hanging in its place.

In Fig. 3 is shown a gauntlet of the seventeenth century with separately articulated fingers. This gauntlet may be molded in one piece, except the thumb and fingers, which must be made separately and fastened with the thumb shield to the leather glove that is attached to the inside of the gauntlet, the same as in Fig. 2.

A breastplate and tassets of the sixteenth century are shown in Fig. 4. The tassets are separate and attached to the front plate with straps and buckles, as shown in the sketch. There is a belt around the waist which helps to hold the back plate on. Attached to the back of the plate would be two short straps at the shoulder. These are passed through the buckles shown at the top right and left-hand corners of the front plate. For decorative purposes the back plate need not be made, and therefore it is not described. The method of making armor is

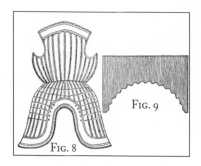

Fig. 8

Fig. 9

Corrugated Breastplate and Former

the same as of making helmets, but as larger pieces are formed it is well to use less clay owing to the bulk and weight.

An arrangement is shown in Fig. 5 to reduce the amount of clay used. This triangular-shaped support, which can be made in any size, is placed on the modeling board or bench and covered with clay. This will make the model light and easy to move around, and will require less clay. It is not necessary to have smooth boards; the rougher the better, as the surface will hold the clay. The clay forms modeled up ready to receive the patches of brown paper on the surface are shown in Figs. 6 and 7.

A German fluted armor used at the beginning of the sixteenth century is shown in Fig. 8. The breastplate and tassets of this armor are supposed to be in one piece, but for convenience in making it will be found best to make them separately and then glue them together after they are taken from the model. A narrow leather belt placed around the armor will cover the joint. Fluted armor takes its name from a series of corrugated grooves, ½ in. in depth, running down the plate. A piece of board, cut into the shape shown in Fig. 9, will be very useful for marking out the fluted lines.

HOME-MADE HAND VISE

A vise for holding small articles while filing can be made as shown in the illustration. The vise consists of three pieces of wood, two for the jaws and one a wedge.

The hinge for connecting the two jaws is made of four small screw eyes, two in each jaw. When locating the place for the screw eyes, place the two in one jaw so they will fit between the two of the other jaw. Put a nail through the eyes when the jaws are matched together and they are ready for the wedge in clamping the article to be filed.—Contributed by John G. Buxton, Redondo Beach, Calif.

Imitation Arms and Armor Part—III

Maces and battle-axes patterned after and made in imitation of the ancient weapons which were used from the fourteenth to the sixteenth century produce fine ornaments for the hall or den, says the English Mechanic. The imitation articles are made of wood, the steel parts represented by tinfoil stuck on with glue and the ornaments carved out with a carving tool.

An English mace used about the middle of the fifteenth century is shown in Fig. 1. The entire length of this weapon is about 24 in.; the handle is round with a four-sided sharp spike extending out from the points of six triangular shaped wings. Cut the handle and spike from one piece of wood

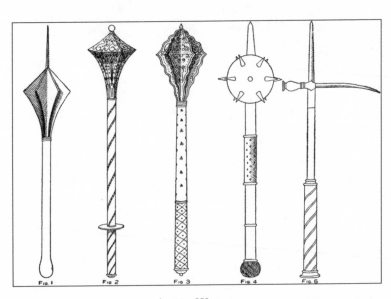

Fig. 1   Fig. 2   Fig. 3   Fig. 4   Fig. 5

Ancient Weapons

and glue the wings on at equal distances apart around the base of the spike. The two bands or wings can be made by gluing two pieces of rope around the handle and fastening it with tacks. These rings can be carved out, but they are somewhat difficult to make. After the glue is dry, remove all the surplus that has been pressed out from the joints with the point of a sharp knife blade and then sandpaper the surface of the wood to make it smooth. Secure some tinfoil to cover the parts in imitation of steel. A thin coat of glue is quickly applied to the surface of the wood and the tinfoil laid on evenly so there will be no wrinkles and without making any more seams than is necessary. The entire weapon, handle and all, is to appear as steel.

An engraved iron mace of the fifteenth century is shown in Fig. 2. This weapon is about 22 in. long, mounted with an eight-sided or octagonal head. It will be easier to make this mace in three pieces, the octagonal head in one piece and the handle in two parts, so that the circular shield shown at the lower end of the handle can be easily placed between the parts. The circular piece or shield can be cut from a piece of wood about ¼ in. thick. The circle is marked out with a compass. A hole is made through the center for the dowel of the two handle parts when they are put together. A wood peg about 2 in. long serves as the dowel. A hole is bored in the end of both handle pieces and these holes well coated with glue, the wood peg inserted in one of them, the shield put on in place and handle parts put together and left for the glue to set. The head is fastened on the end of the handle with a dowel in the same manner as putting the handle parts together.

The head must have a pattern sketched upon each side in pencil marks, such as ornamental scrolls, leaves, flowers, etc. These ornaments must be carved out to a depth of about ¼ in. with a sharp carving tool. If such a tool is not at hand, or the amateur cannot use it well, an excellent substitute will be found in using a sharp-pointed and red-hot poker, or pieces of heavy wire heated to burn out the pattern to the desired depth. The handle also has a scroll to be engraved. When the whole is finished and cleaned up, it is covered with tinfoil in imitation of steel. The tinfoil should be applied carefully, as before mentioned, and firmly pressed into the engraved parts with the finger tips or thumb.

A French mace used in the sixteenth century is shown in Fig. 3. This weapon is about 22 in. long and has a wood handle covered with dark red cloth or velvet, the lower part to have a gold or red silk cord wound around it, as shown, the whole handle finished off with small brass-headed nails. The top has six ornamental carved wings which are cut out, fastened on

the handle and covered with tinfoil, as described in Fig. 2.

Figure 4 shows a Morning Star which is about 26 in. long. The spiked ball and the four-sided and sharp-pointed spike are of steel. The ball may be made of clay or wood and covered with tinfoil. The spikes are cut out of wood, sharp-pointed and cone-shaped, the base having a brad to stick into the ball. The wood spikes are also covered with tinfoil. The handle is of steel imitation, covered in the middle with red cloth or velvet and studded with large-headed steel nails.

A war hammer of the fifteenth century is shown in Fig. 5. Its length is about 3 ft.

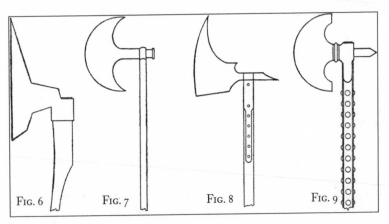

FIG. 6   FIG. 7   FIG. 8   FIG. 9

Battle Axes of the Fourteenth, Fifteenth and Sixteenth Centuries

The lower half of the handle is wood, covered with red velvet, with a golden or yellow cord wound spirally over the cloth. The upper half of the handle is steel, also, the hammer and spike. The entire handle should be made of one piece, then the hammer put on the base of the spike. The spike made with a peg in its lower end and well glued, can be firmly placed in position by the peg fitting in a hole made for its reception in the top of the handle. Finish up the steel parts with tinfoil.

The following described weapons can be constructed of the same materials and built up in the same way as described in the foregoing articles: A horseman's short-handled battle-axe, used at the end of the fifteenth century, is shown in Fig. 6. The handle is of wood and the axe in imitation steel. Figure 7 shows an English horseman's battle-axe used at the beginning of the reign of Queen Elizabeth. The handle and axe both are to be shown in steel. A German foot soldier's poleaxe used at the end of the fourteenth century is shown in Fig. 8. The handle is made of dark wood and the axe covered with tinfoil. Figure 9 shows an English foot soldier's jedburgh axe of the sixteenth century. The handle is of wood, studded with large brass or steel nails. The axe is shown in steel. All of these axes are about the same length.

KITES OF MANY KINDS AND HOW TO MAKE THEM

One of the prettiest of all is the butterfly kite. To make this get two thin kite sticks of equal length. Bend each in an arc, tying one end of a strong string to one end of each stick and the other end of the string to a point about 3 in. from the other end of the stick. This leaves one end of each stick free, hooking over the hemisphere described by the thread and the stick. Now tie another thread to each of these free ends and tie the other end of the thread to a point near the other end of the stick, corresponding with the distance from the end at which the first strings were tied on the opposite side. This done, you should have two arched frames, each an exact counterpart of the other in size, curvature and

Boy Kite

weight. Now fasten the two frames together so that the arcs will overlap each other as shown in the sketch. Bind the intersecting points securely with thread. To make the butterfly's head, secure two heavy broom straws or two short wires, and attach them to the top part of the wing frames near where the sticks intersect, so that the straws or wires will cross. These form the antennae, or the "smellers". Then select the color of paper you want, yellow, brown, blue, white or any other color; lay it on a flat surface and place the frame on top of it, holding the frame

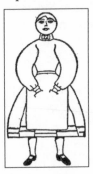

Girl Kite

down securely with a weight. Then with a pair of scissors cut the paper around the frame, leaving about a ½-in. margin for pasting. Cut slits in the paper about 2 in. apart around the curves and at all angles to keep the paper from wrinkling when it is pasted. Distribute the paste with a small brush and make the overlaps a little more than ¼ in. wide and press them together with a soft cloth. When the kite is dry decorate it with paint or strips of colored paper in any design you may fancy. The best effects are produced by pasting pieces of colored paper on top of the other paper. Black paper decorations show up to fine advantage when the kite is in flight. Attach the "belly-band" to the curved sticks by punching a hole in the paper in the same manner as it is attached to the common hexagonal or coffin-shaped kite. With a tail, your kite is ready to fly.

Another interesting design is the boy kite. With light colored coat and vest and gay striped trousers, the kite standing high in the air always attracts attention and affords splendid sport for the American youth in springtime.

In making a boy kite it should be remembered that the larger the boy is the better he

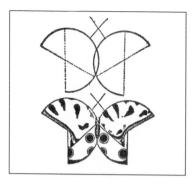

Butterfly Kite

column, and crossed so that the other ends are 3ft. apart. Tack them and the arm stick together at the point where they intersect. Small hoops and cross stick of the same material as the head frame should be fastened to both extremities of the arm stick and the lower ends of the leg stick for

will fly. To construct the frame, two straight sticks, say 3½ ft. long, should serve for the legs and body; another straight stick forms the spine and should be about 2 ft. 4 in. long. For the arms, get a fourth straight stick about 3 ft. 3 in. long. Make the frame for the head by bending a light tough stick in a circle about 7 in. in diameter. Bind it tightly with a strong thread and through its center run the spine. Then tack on the arm stick 3 in. under the circle so that the spinal column crosses the arm stick exactly in the center. Wrap tightly with strong thread and tack on the two sticks that are to serve for the legs and body. The leg sticks should be fastened to the arm stick about 6 in. on either side of the spinal

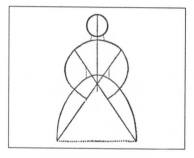

Frame for Girl Kite

the hands and feet. See that both hand frames are exactly alike and exercise equal caution regarding the foot frames; also see that the arm stick is at exact right angles with the spine stick and that the kite joints are all firmly tied and the kite evenly balanced; otherwise it may be lopsided. Fasten on the strings of the frame, beginning at the neck at equal distances from the spines, as indicated by the dotted lines in the diagram.

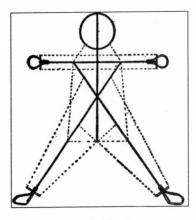

Frame for Boy Kite

Extend a string slantingly from the armstick to the head on both sides of the spinal column, and run all the other strings as shown in the cut, being careful that both sides of the frame correspond in measurements.

To cover the kite, select different colors of papers to suit your taste, and after pasting them together, lay the paper on the floor and placing the frame on it, cut out the pattern. Leave an edge of ½ in. all around and make a slit in this edge every 6 in. and at each angle; make the slits 2 in. part around the head. After the kite is pasted and dry, paint the buttons, hair, eyes, hands, feet, etc., as you desire. Arrange the "belly band" and tail band and attach the kite string in the same manner as in the ordinary coffin-shaped kite.

The "lady kite" is made on the same principle as the boy kite. The frame may be made exactly as the boy kite and then "dressed" with tissue paper to represent a girl, or it may be made on the special frame, page 81. Remember the dotted lines represent the strings or thread, and the other lines indicate the kite sticks. Be careful with your measurements so that each side of the kite corresponds exactly and is well balanced. Also see that every point where the sticks intersect is firmly tacked and bound.

To cover the kite, first paste together pieces of tissue paper of different color to suit your taste. The paste should be made of flour and water and boiled. Make the seams or overlaps not quite ⅜ in. wide. Lay the paper on the floor, using weights to hold it down, and place the frame of the kite upon it. Then cut out the paper around the frame, leaving an edge of ½ in. Don't forget to make a slit in the edge every 6 or 7 in. and at each angle. Around the head the slits are cut 2 in. apart, as in the case of the boy kite. After the kite is dry, paint the paper as your fancy dictates.

To make the breast band, punch notes through the paper, one upon each side of the leg sticks just above the bottom, and one upon with side of the arm sticks at the shoulder. Run one end of the string through the hole at the leg stick; tie the other end at the right shoulder. Fasten one end of another string of the same length at the bottom of the right leg; pass the string up across the first band and tie the other end at the left shoulder. Attach the kite string to the breast band at then point where the two strings intersect. Tie the knot so that you can slide the kite string up or down until it is properly adjusted. The tail band is made by tying a string to the leg sticks at the bottom of the breast band. Let the string hang slack below the skirt and attach rules apply in attaching the string and tail to the boy kite.

You can make the lady look as if dancing and kicking in the clouds by making the feet of stiff pasteboard and allowing them to hang loose from the line which forms the bottom of the skirt. The feet will move and sway with each motion of the kite.

TOY DARTS AND PARACHUTES

A dart (Fig. 1) is made of a cork having a tin cap, a needle and some feathers. The needle is run through the center cork A and a pin or piece of steel is put through the eye of he needle. Take a quantity of small feathers, B, and tie them together securely at the bottom. Bore a hole in the center of the cap C, and fasten the feathers inside of it. Fasten the cap on the cork and the dart is ready for use. When throwing the dart at a target stand from 6 to 10 ft. away from it.

The parachute is made by cutting a piece of paper 15 in. square and tying a piece of

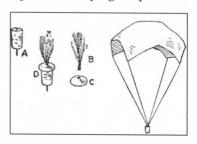

Dart Parts and Paper Parachute

paper 15 in. square and tying a piece of string to each corner. The strings should be about 15 in. long. Tie all four strings together in a knot at the end and fasten them in the top of a cork with a small tack. It is best to be as high as possible when flying the parachute as the air currents will sail it high and fast. Take hold of the parachute by the cork and run it through the air with the wind, letting it go at arm's length.—Contributed by J. Gordon Dempsey, Paterson, N. J.

WINTER FUN WITH SLEDS AND SNOW

A HANDY ICE CHISEL

Fishing through the ice is great sport, but cutting the first holes preparatory to setting the lines is not always an easy task. The ice chisel here described will be found very handy, and may be made at very slight expense.

In the top of an old ax-head drill a ⁹⁄₁₆-in. hole, and then tap it for a ⅜-in. gas-pipe, about 18 in. long. Thread the other end of the pipe, and screw on an old snow-shovel handle. When ready for use, screw the two pieces together and you have your chisel complete.

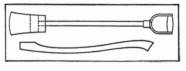

Combination Ax and Ice Chisel

A short ax-handle may be included in the outfit. When the holes are finished and your lines set, unscrew the pipe from the head of the ax, put in the handle, and your ax is ready to cut the wood to keep your fire going.—Contributed by C. J. Rand, West Somerville, Mass.

A HOME-MADE YANKEE BOBSLED

A good coasting sled, which I call a Yankee bob, can be made from two hardwood barrel staves, two pieces of 2 by 6-in. pine, a piece of hardwood for the rudder and a few pieces of boards. The 2 by 6-in. pieces should be a little longer than one-third the length of the staves, and each piece cut tapering from the widest part, 6 in., down to 2 in., and then

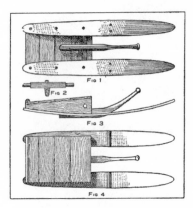

Runners Made of Barrel Staves

and a lag screw put through and turned in the rudder piece, making it so the rudder will turn right and left and, also, up and down. Two cleats are nailed to the upper sides of the runners and in the middle lengthways for the person's heels to rest against.

Any child can guide this bob, as all he has to do is to guide the rudder right and left to go in the direction named. If he wants to stop, he pulls up on the handle and the heel of the rudder will dig into the snow, causing too much friction for the sled to go any further.— Contributed by Wm. Algie, Jr., Little Falls, N. Y.

fastened to the staves with large wood screws as shown in Fig. 1. Boards 1 in. thick are nailed on top of the pieces for a seat and to hold the runners together. The boards should be of such a length as to make the runners about 18 in. apart.

A 2-in. shaft of wood, Fig. 2, is turned down to 1 in. on the ends and put through holes that must be bored in the front ends of the 2 by 6-in. pieces. A small pin is put through each end of the shaft to keep it in place. The rudder is a 1½-in. hardwood piece which should be tapered to ½ in. at the bottom and shod with a thin piece of iron. A ½-in. hole is bored through the center of the shaft

COASTERS AND CHAIR SLEIGHS

Make your own sled, boys! There is no use in buying them, because your hand-made sled is probably better than any purchased one and then you can take so much more pride in it when you know it is of

Chair Sleigh

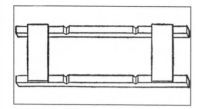

Folding Chair Sleigh Open

Folding Chair Sleigh Bottom

your own construction. There are so many different designs of sleds that can be made by hand that the matter can be left almost entirely to your own ingenuity. You can make one like the bought sleds and face the runners with pieces of an iron hoop which will answer every purpose. A good sled for coasting consists simply of two barrel staves and three pieces of board as shown in the picture, Fig. 1. No bought sled will equal it for coasting and it is also just the thing for carrying loads of snow for building snow houses. The method of its construction is so simple that no other description is needed than the picture. You can make a chair-sleigh out of this by fitting a chair on the cross board instead of the long top board or it will be still stronger if the top board is allowed to remain, and then you will have a device that can

readily again be transformed into a coasting sled. In making the chair-sleigh it is necessary, in order to hold the chair in place, to nail four L-shaped blocks on the cross boards, one for each leg of the chair. Shating along over the ice and pushing the chair in front of him the proud possessor of a chair-sleigh may take his mother, grown sister or lady friend with him on his outings, and permit her to ride in the chair.

FOLDING CHAIR SLEIGH

A folding chair sleigh is even more enjoyable and convenient than the device just described. If the ice pond is far from home this may be placed under your arm and carried where you like.

The illustrations, Figs. 2 and 3, show all the parts as they should look before being joined together. The seat may be made of a piece of canvas or carpet.

Folding Chair Sleigh Closed

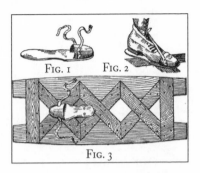

Fig. 1　Fig. 2

Fig. 3

Made from Barrel Staves

The hinges are of leather. Figure 4 shows the folding chair sleigh after it has been put together. Skates are employed for the runners. The skates may be strapped on or taken off whenever desired. When the chair is lifted the supports slip from the notches on the side bars and fall on the runner bars. The chair is then folded up so that it can be carried by a small boy. With regular metal hinges and light timbers a very handsome chair can be constructed that will also afford an ornamental lawn chair for summer.

HOMEMADE SNOWSHOES

Secure four light barrel staves and sandpaper the outside smooth. Take two old shoes that are extra large and cut off the tops and heels so as to leave only the toe covering fastened to the sole. Purchase two long book straps, cut them in two in the middle and fasten the ends on the toe covering, as shown in Fig. 1. The straps are used to attach the snowshoe to the regular shoe. When buckling up the straps be sure to leave them loose enough for the foot to work freely, Fig. 2. Fasten the barrel staves in pairs, leaving a space of 4 in. between them as shown in Fig. 3, with thin strips of wood. Nail the old shoe soles to crosspieces placed one-third of the way from one end as shown.—Contributed by David Brown, Kansas City, Mo.

HOW TO MAKE A BICYCLE COASTING SLED

The accompanying drawing and sketch illustrate a new type of coasting sled built on the bicycle principle. This coaster is simple and easy to make, says

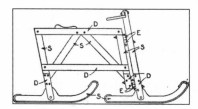

Has the Lines of a Bicycle

Scientific American. It is constructed of a good quality of pine. The pieces marked S are single, and should be about 1 by 1½ in.; the pieces marked D are double or in duplicate, and should be ½ by 1½ in. The runners are shod with iron and are pivoted to the uprights as shown, double pieces being secured to the uprights to make a fork. The seat is a board,

Coasting

to the underside of which is a block, which drops down between the two top slats and is secured with a pin. A footrest is provided consisting of a short crosspiece secured to the front of the frame and resting on the two lower slats. The frame and front short eyebolts, E, with a short bolt through each pair as shown.

How to Make an Eskimo Snow House

by George E. Walsh

Playing in the snow can be raised to a fine art if boys and girls will build their creations with some attempt at architectural skill and not content themselves with mere rough work. Working in snow and ice opens a wide field for an expression of taste and invention, but the construction of houses and forts out of this plastic material provides the greatest amount of pleasure to the normally healthy boy or girl.

The snow house of the Eskimo is probably the unhealthiest of buildings made by any savage to live in, but it makes an excellent playhouse

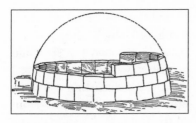

Laying the Snow Bricks

can be used, according to size of the house and thickness of the walls.

First, the snow blocks must be packed and pressed firmly into position out of moist snow that will pack. A very light, dry snow will not pack easily, and it may be necessary to use a little water. If the snow is of the right consistency, there will be no trouble in packing and working with it. As most of the blocks are to be of the same size throughout, it will pay to make a mold for them by forming a box of old boards nailed together, minus the top, and with a movable bottom, or rather no bottom at all. Place the four-sided box on a flat board and ram snow in it, forcing it down closely. Then by lifting the box up and tapping the box from above, the block will drop out. In this way blocks of uniform size are formed, which makes the building simpler and easier.

While one boy makes the blocks another can shave them off at the edges and two others can build the house, one inside of the circle and the other outside. The Eskimos build their

in winter, and represents at the same time a most ingenious employment of the arch system in building. The Eskimos build their snow houses without the aid of any scaffolding or interior falsework, and while there is a keystone at the top of the dome, it is not essential to the support of the walls. These are self-supporting from the time the first snow blocks are put down until the last course is laid.

The snow house is of the beehive shape and the ground plan is that of a circle. The circle is first laid out on the ground and a space cleared for it. Then a row of snow blocks is laid on the ground and another course of similar blocks placed on top. The snow blocks are not exactly square in shape, but about 12 in. long, 6 in. high and 4 or 5 in. thick. Larger or smaller blocks snow houses in this way, and the man inside stays there until he is completely walled in. Then the door and a window are cut through the wall.

Each layer of snow blocks must have a slight slant at the top toward the center so that the walls will constantly curve inward. This slant at the top is obtained better by slicing off the lower surfaces of each block before putting it in its course. The top will then have a uniform inward slant.

The first course of the snow house should be thicker than the others, and the thickness of the walls gradually decreases toward the top. A wall, however, made of 6-in. blocks throughout will hold up a snow house perfectly, if its top is no more than 6 or 7 ft. above the ground.

If a higher house is needed the walls should be thicker at the base and well up toward the middle.

The builder has no mortar for binding the blocks together, and therefore he must make his joints smooth and even and force in loose snow to fill up the crevices. A little experience will enable one to do this work well, and the construction of the house will proceed rapidly. The Eskimos build additions to their houses by adding various dome-shaped structures to one side, and the young architect can imitate them. Such dome-shaped structures are shown in one of the illustrations.

A fact not well understood and appreciated is that the Eskimo beehive snow house represents true arch building.

Three-Room Snow House

It requires no scaffolding in building and it exerts no outward thrust. In the ordinary keystone arch used by builders, a temporary structure must be erected to hold the walls up until the keystone is fitted in position, and the base must be buttressed against an outward thrust. The Eskimo does not have to consider these points. There is no outward thrust, and the top keystone is not necessary to hold the structure up. It is doubtful whether such an arch could be built of brick or stone without scaffolding, but with the snow blocks it is a simple matter.

MAKING SKIS AND SKI-TOBOGGANS

During the winter months everyone is thinking of skating, coasting or ski-running and jumping. Those too timid to run down a hill standing upright on skis must take their pleasure in coasting or skating.

The ordinary ski can be made into a coasting ski-toboggan by joining two pairs together with bars without injury to their use for running and jumping. The ordinary factory-made skis cost from $2.50 per pair up, but any boy can make an excellent pair for 50 cents.

In making a pair of skis, select two strips of Norway pine free from knots, 1 in. thick, 4 in. wide and 7 or 8 ft. long. Try to procure as fine and straight a grain as possible. The pieces are dressed thin at both ends leaving about 1 ft. in the center the full thickness of 1 in., and gradually thinning to a scant ½ in. at the ends. One end of each piece is tapered to a point beginning 12 in. from the end.

A groove is cut on the under side, about ¼ in. wide and ⅛ in. deep, and running almost the full length of the ski. This will make it track straight and tends to prevent side slipping. The shape of each piece for a ski, as it appears before bending, is shown in Fig. 1.

The pointed end of each piece is placed in boiling water for at least 1 hour, after which the pieces are ready for bending. The bend is made on an ordinary stepladder. The pointed ends are stuck under the back of one step and the other end securely tied to the ladder, as shown in Fig. 2. They should remain tied to the ladder 48 hours in a moderate temperature, after which they will hold their shape permanently.

The two straps, Fig. 3, are nailed on a little forward of the center of gravity so that when the foot is lifted, the front of the ski will be raised. Tack on a piece of sheepskin or deer hide where the foot rests, Fig. 4.

The best finish for skis is boiled linseed oil. After two or three applications the under side will take a polish like glass from the contact with the snow.

The ski-toboggan is made by placing two pairs of skis together side by side and fastening them with two bars across the top. The bars are held

Fig. 1   Fig. 2

Forming the Skis

The Toe Straps

Ski-Toboggan

with V-shaped metal clips as shown in Fig. 5.—Contributed by Frank Scobie, Sleepy Eye, Minn.

PECULIAR PROPERTIES OF ICE

Of all the boys who make snowballs probably few know what occurs during the process. Under ordinary conditions water turns to ice when the temperature falls to 32°, but when in motion, or under pressure, much lower temperatures are required to make it a solid. In the same way, ice which is somewhat below the freezing point can be made liquid by applying pressure, and will remain liquid until the pressure is removed, when it will again return to its original state. Snow, being simply finely divided ice, becomes liquid in places when compressed by the hands, and when the pressure is removed the liquid portions solidify and unite all the particles in one mass. In extremely cold weather it is almost impossible to make a snowball, because a greater amount of pressure is then required to make the snow liquid.

This process of melting and freezing under different pressures and a constant temperature is well illustrated by the experiment shown in Figs. 1, 2 and 3. A block of ice, A, Fig. 1, is supported at each end by boxes BB, and a weight, W, is hung on a wire loop which

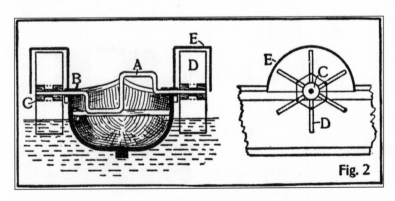

Detail of Paddle Boat

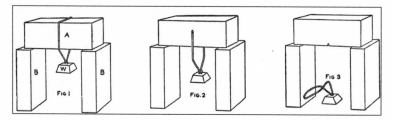

Experiment with a Block of Ice

passes around the ice as shown. The pressure of the wire will then melt the ice and allow the wire to sink down through the ice as shown in Fig. 2. The wire will continue to cut its way through the ice until it passes all the way through the piece, as shown in Fig. 3. This experiment not only illustrates how ice melts under pressure, but also how it solidifies when the pressure is removed, for the block will still be left in one piece after the wire has passed through.

Another peculiar property of ice is its tendency to flow. It may seem strange that ice should flow like water, but the glaciers of Switzerland and other countries are literally rivers of ice. The snow which accumulates on the mountains in vast quantities is turned to ice as a result of the enormous pressure caused by its own weight, and flows through the natural channels it has made in the rock until it reaches the valley below. In flowing through these channels it frequently passes around bends, and when two branches come together the bodies of ice unite the same as water would under the same conditions. The rate of flow is often very slow; sometimes only one or two feet a day, but, no matter how slow the motion may be, the large body of ice has to bend in moving.

This property of ice is hard to illustrate with the substance itself, but may be clearly shown by sealing-wax, which resembles ice in this respect. Any attempt to bend a piece of cold sealing-wax with the hands results in breaking it, but by placing it between books, or supporting it in some similar way, it will gradually change from the original shape A, and assume the shape shown at B.

THE RUNNING SLEIGH

Another winter sport, very popular in Sweden, and which has already reached America, is the running sleigh," shown in the illustration. A light sleigh is equipped with long double runners and is propelled by foot power. The person using the sleigh stands with one foot upon a rest attached to one of the braces connecting the runners and propels the sleigh by pushing backward with the other foot. To steady the body an upright support is attached to the runners. The contrivance can be used upon hard frozen ground, thin ice and snow-covered surfaces, and under favorable conditions moves with remarkable speed. The "running sleigh" has a decided advantage over skis, because the two foot supports are braced so that they cannot come apart. Any boy can make the sleigh.

THE TOBOGGAN SLED

When the snow is very deep a toboggan sled is the thing for real sport. The runners of the ordinary sled break through the crust of the deep snow, blocking the progress, and spoiling the fun. The toboggan sled, with its broad, smooth bottom, glides along over the soft surface with perfect ease.

To make the toboggan sled, secure two boards each 10 ft. long and 1 ft. wide and so thin that they can be easily bent. Place the boards beside each other and join them together with cross sticks. Screw the boards to the cross stick from

Running Sleigh

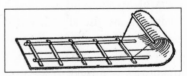

The Toboggan

the bottom and be sure that the heads of the screws are buried deep enough in the wood to not protrude, so that the bottom will present an absolutely smooth surface to the snow. Fasten two side bars to the top of the cross sticks and screw them firmly. In some instances the timbers are fastened together by strings, a groove being cut in the bottom of the boards so as to keep the strings from protruding and being ground to pieces. After the side bars are securely fastened, bend the ends of the boards over and tie them to the ends of the front cross bar to hold them in position. See Fig. 6. The strings for keeping the boards bent must be very strong. Pieces of stout wire, or a slender steel rod, are even better. The toboggan slide is the favored device of sport among the boys in Canada, where nearly every boy knows how to make them.